Manage Your Time
Your Work
Yourself

Manage Your Time
Your Work
Yourself

The Updated Edition

Merrill E. Douglass
Donna N. Douglass

American Management Association

New York • Atlanta • Boston • Chicago • Kansas City • San Francisco • Washington, D.C.
Brussels • Toronto • Mexico City

This book is available at a special
discount when ordered in bulk quantities.
For information, contact Special Sales Department,
AMACOM, a division of American Management Association,
135 West 50th Street, New York, NY 10020.

Library of Congress Cataloging-in-Publication Data

Douglass, Merrill E.
      Manage your time, your work, yourself / Merrill E. Douglass, Donna
  N. Douglass. —Updated ed.
          p.   cm.
      Includes index.
      ISBN 0-8144-7825-5
      1. Time management. 2. Success. I. Douglass, Donna N.
  II. Title.
  HD69.T54D68   1993
  650.1—dc20   92-37820
                                                           CIP

Printing number

10 9 8 7 6 5 4 3 2 1

To
Mary Cobb Bugg,
who started it all

Contents

Contents

List of Figures

Preface

We've been helping people manage time better since 1972. That was the year we founded the Time Management Center. It all began with a phone call from Mary Cobb Bugg, director of Community Educational Services at Emory University in Atlanta, Georgia. She was looking for someone to develop and conduct a time-management seminar. Merrill was the newest management professor at the Emory University Business School, and the last one she had called. Every other professor had turned her down. That first seminar was very successful, and, as the saying goes, the rest is history. Over 2,000 seminars later, we're still going strong.

We wrote our first book, *Manage Your Time, Manage Your Work, Manage Yourself,* in 1980, identifying many of the problems and solutions as we saw them then. Naturally, we've changed over the years, and we've continued to learn more about good time management. That's the reason for this book . . . to share what we've been learning with our readers.

This book is intended to help you become an excellent time master. A new and unique feature is the Time-Management Profile, covering several different aspects of managing time. The Profile allows readers to assess their own personal time-management strengths and weaknesses. This will help identify potential improvements and indicate possible starting points. Within the book, we describe hundreds of practical ideas and techniques for building good time habits.

We believe that the concepts we write about can literally change your life . . . if you apply them. In other words, they work, if you do. Since 1972, we've conducted seminars in hundreds of companies all over the world. Thousands of people have tested and proven the value of these ideas. We believe they will work just as well for you as they have for others.

Finally, we'd love to hear how our ideas help you most. Please write and tell us. Perhaps your story will appear in a future book.

Best wishes for good times ahead.

Manage Your Time
Your Work
Yourself

One
Facing the Daily Dilemma

Time—all men neglect it; all regret the loss of it; nothing can be done without it.

Voltaire

Most people face a daily dilemma: too much to do and not enough time to do it in. There are too many opportunities to pursue, too many problems to solve, too many projects to work on, too many calls to return, too many people wanting too many pieces of your time. Our friend Mark puts it this way: "If a great day is defined as one where you get everything done, then I haven't had a great day for years."

Dealing With Too Little Time

Is there a secret formula that will make it all work? Can you make the pieces fit? Can you find the time for everything? In an act of pure desperation, some of us go to extremes in our efforts to fit it all in. A few strategies deserve special mention because they are so common—and so notoriously nonproductive.

Working Faster

First, we try to step up the pace and do everything faster, like speeding up a movie. We assume that with this hurry-up approach we can surely finish everything. To be sure, there are occasions when working faster makes sense. If we are working at a lazy pace and taking more time than we need to get the job done, working faster can be valuable.

But most often, working faster only produces more problems.

Under rushed conditions, we make more mistakes. The faster we go, the more mistakes we make—mistakes which require additional time to be fixed. When hurrying, we have even less time to think, plan, and reflect before acting. Guilt rises and we feel superficial as we skim through issues that we know deserve more time. Tempers flare; ulcers develop; blood pressure soars. The days are even more frenzied than before.

Getting Organized

A second approach is to try to get better organized. In endless pursuit of organization, the stressed-out man or woman may decide to buy a notebook organizer/planner system. This system will be *the answer*. After all, that's what the ad promised! A new product appears almost every month. Some people even have a collection of such systems.

There is some value in this approach. Many people are, indeed, poorly organized and fail to plan well. If it is used regularly, a good notebook organizer can certainly help fine-tune organizing skills. However, even some who have mastered these systems still wind up short, with unmet expectations. They become good "bookkeepers" but still face the frustration of things left undone.

Working Longer

When working faster and getting better organized don't work, there may appear to be only one strategy left: working longer. Weekly workweeks stretch into fifty, sixty, seventy, or even more hours. Personal time disappears as work time increases. Fatigue—both physical and mental—becomes a factor. Judgment is less clear. Hours are spent trying to solve problems that a fresh mind could solve in minutes.

In the short run, working longer seems to work. You really might get more done, at least on the job. However, the problem may worsen at home because you have even fewer personal hours. Even on the job, the benefits are usually short-lived. Although longer hours have become the rule, you discover that there is still more that could be done.

If these are poor time-management strategies, why do we keep using them? Probably because we believe these approaches will help us accomplish everything we think needs to be done. When your back is up against the wall, you *have* to do something!

We fail to realize that, no matter how much we do, there is always more to be done. We doom ourselves to a life of frustration, disillusionment, and disappointment. We simply cannot do everything. No matter how fast we work, there are only twenty-four hours a day. No matter how organized we are, there are only twenty-four hours a day. No matter how long we work, we can't work more than twenty-four hours a day.

There is only one solution: choices. Since you can't do everything, you must choose what you will do, and what you will not do. With too much to do and too little time, choice is the only possible alternative.

Always Being Busy

Time is a paradox. We never seem to have enough time, yet we have all the time there is. The problem is not a shortage of time, but how we choose to use the time available to us.

An old American proverb says, "You sometimes have to do less in order to get more done." For some reason though, many of us are reluctant to slow down until forced to do so. Our lives are dependent on an increasing flurry of activity. To stop is to risk collapse, but to continue is insane.

An ancient Chinese proverb says, "Besides the noble art of getting things done, there is the noble art of leaving things undone. The wisdom of life consists in eliminating the nonessentials."

Do you agree with the Chinese proverb? Do you really think of leaving things undone as a noble art? Most of us don't. We think that being busy is a virtue and the busier the better. When things are left undone, we feel guilty and frustrated. We want to do more, not less. Most of us just keep adding activities to our lives; we seldom subtract. We argue that it's all important; it all has to be done.

Yet, the inevitable truth is that you can't do everything. Accept this as fact. Stop living as though the world will stop turning without you. It won't. Once you do this, you have taken a big step toward becoming an effective time manager. "The wisdom of life is the elimination of nonessentials." Maybe that is the missing key. Make sure that what is left over are the nonessentials. Leave essentials undone, and you have problems. However, leave nonessentials undone, and nothing happens. Trouble is, we don't always know what they are.

Life is a simple duality, essentials and nonessentials. Things to do, and things to not do. We focus all our attention on what to do, but we spend very little time deciding what *not* to do with our time. Most of us make a to-do list, but have you ever made a not-to-do list? Perhaps you should; just having such a list can help. Not everything has to be done, only certain essentials. We can safely ignore the nonessentials.

The hard part, of course, is to separate essentials from non-essentials. They don't usually come neatly labeled. But maybe it would be easier if we forced ourselves to actually *put* a label on them. How? Make two lists. Call one "Essentials" and the other "Nonessentials." Whenever you put something on the Essentials list, write an explanation of why it is essential. If you can honestly justify it—in writing—it's in. Otherwise, throw that time-eating activity out.

Failure to identify and drop all the nonessentials from our lives exposes us to severe risk. We clutter up our world with junk and problems. Pausing now and then to clean out the closets of our lives is a refreshing, therapeutic exercise. By doing so, we learn to focus on what really matters. Once we honestly do this, we can stop worrying about the nonessentials we no longer have time or energy to consider. We can focus our attention on the truly important issues.

Understanding Our Own Personal Temperament

Time management is really self-management. Although time is not adaptable, people are. Managing time means adapting ourselves to its passage in some appropriate, satisfying manner. It means managing ourselves. If time seems to be out of control, it means that we are out of control. To bring ourselves back under control, we must learn new, more appropriate habits. That means we must change. Ouch! The thought of changing can send shivers down the spine of the faint-hearted, but change is necessary anyway. We must grin and bear it until we learn to love it.

Personal temperament complicates the issue of time (or self-) management. In our last book, we discussed in great detail how temperament and personality style affect time management (Merrill Douglass and Donna Douglass, *Time Management for Teams*, New York: AMACOM, 1992). We refer those readers who want a more complete explanation than the following summary to our book.

The concept is simple: Everyone is a blend of four basic temperaments. Throughout the ages, these four temperaments have been called many things, but a simple description, using the ancient Greek labels, would be like this:

Choleric:	Take charge, dominant, aggressive, basic aim in life is to get things done.
Sanguine:	Outgoing, talkative, likes people, basic aim in life is to have fun.
Melancholy:	Intense, contemplative, detailed, basic aim in life is to do things right.

Phlegmatic: Quiet, pleasant, agreeable, basic aim in life is to take it easy.

While you have some aspects of all four temperaments in your personality, one will usually be primary, one secondary, and the other two rather weak. How the four temperaments blend together defines your personality style. Your environment and experiences help determine how you express your temperament in actual behavior.

Naturally, your temperament affects your relationship with time, just as it affects everything else you do. For some, time management comes almost naturally; for others, it is more difficult, almost contrary to their natural tendencies. Some temperaments enjoy change; others almost dread it. The key is to understand both the strengths and weaknesses of your particular temperament.

Attitudes Toward Change and Control

To change successfully, we must also *believe* that we can change. We must *believe* that what we do will make a difference. In the movie *The Empire Strikes Back*, Jodi told Luke Skywalker how to raise his ship from the mire with his mental powers. Luke tried and failed. Then Jodi showed him how. As the ship arose from the mire, Luke cried, "I don't believe it!" Jodi answered simply, "That is why you fail."

Psychologists in recent years have analyzed people's attitudes toward controlling their environment. At one extreme are the "internals," people who believe strongly that they can make a difference in their world. Although they may not be able to control everything, they believe they can at least have an impact on the significant things that happen to them.

At the other extreme are the "externals," people who believe they are at the mercy of their environment. They believe they have no control or influence over the things that happen to them. They feel pushed around. They simply react to their environment—and usually complain about what happens to them.

Everyone falls somewhere along this external-internal continuum. The closer you are to the internal side, the more likely you are to gain control of your time. The closer you are to the external side, the more difficulty you experience. It will be hard for you to gain control of your time, because deep down you feel that it's not possible.

What is your attitude toward control? Look at Figure 1-1, take a

Figure 1-1. Attitudes toward control.

External				Internal
I can control nothing in my life.	I can control a few things in my environment.	I have control over a lot of things, but there are many things I have no control over.	I can control most of the things in my environment.	I can control everything in my life.

moment for an honest self-analysis, and consider the question seriously. Your answer will be a big clue to whether you will eventually be successful in controlling your time. Where would you place yourself on the external-internal continuum?

The more you believe you can control, the more you will try to control, and the more you will control. Of course, there are certain calamities that none of us can anticipate. However, letting the possibility of such disasters govern our daily behavior is self-defeating. Most of us could probably control far more than we believe we can.

The first step may be to change your thinking. Henry Ford put it this way: "Whether you think you can or you can't, you're right." How right he was! What you think is more important than any objective evaluation of whether you are right or wrong. You usually act in ways that are consistent with your beliefs. To master your time, you must first believe you can do it.

Keeping Up With Today's Fast Pace

Although time management has always been important, it is only in recent years that large numbers of people have devoted much attention to it. Forty years ago there were no books on the subject and only an occasional article. Even twenty years ago there were only two or three books and a handful of articles. Few companies were teaching time management in the 1970s. Now there are hundreds of books and thousands of articles, and every major company teaches it. What has happened to cause these changes?

First, expectations of what people should accomplish in their work have been rising. Every year, your organization expects more from you than it did the year before. Very seldom do people report that this year their organization expects *less* of them than last year!

Second, the business environment has become increasingly complex. Everything is changing. Foreign competition has become a far stronger challenge than we ever dreamed thirty years ago. The entire corporate culture is in upheaval. Total quality management, self-directed work teams, and technological innovations are reshaping the way we think and work. Environmental concerns, changes in tax laws and other legislation, worldwide political upheaval, governmental controls, economic uncertainty, and dozens of similar issues are creating new demands on all of us.

Third, the rate of change gets faster each year. Alvin Toffler called this phenomenon future shock (*Future Shock*, New York: Random House, 1970). Everyone can absorb change to some extent. When the pace of change becomes greater than an individual's ability to cope with it, problems develop. Most of these problems revolve around time issues. Most experts agree that over the next ten years, we will see even more—and faster—changes than ever before.

It's not surprising that these increasing pressures are also felt at the personal level. Individuals who are supposed to oversee and handle all the complexities at work are also demanding more for themselves personally. We want more time for our lives—personal lives we're supposed to have away from our jobs—and we have very high expectations. A recent Hilton Hotel study showed that people are willing to give up as much as 20 percent of their income to gain an extra day a week for themselves. Time has become important to the individual, as well as to the organization.

All these factors—increasing expectations, increasing complexity, and increasing rate of change—have enhanced our awareness of time. We have no more time to achieve results than we did in the past, yet the difficulty involved in doing so has dramatically increased. Rising pressures in all aspects of our lives have forced us to rethink what time means and how we can squeeze the most out of each minute.

In many ways, time management is simply common sense. However, that doesn't make it easy. As Will Rogers frequently observed, "Just because it's common sense doesn't mean it's common practice." There is a huge difference between knowing what to do and actually doing it. Knowing what to do is necessary but not enough. It takes knowledge, desire, and action to turn common sense into common practice for you.

Our primary goal in this book is to help you be successful in every part of your life. We have worked with Time Management since the early 1970s, and we share with you what we have learned. We discuss the important principles of time management, help you examine yourself, and suggest solutions for your specific time problems. By the end of the book, you should have a better understanding of your time problems and a clear plan for action. In addition, we try to add the fire needed to get you moving.

Most of this book focuses on time problems at work. However, the ideas that help solve such problems also help solve personal-time problems. Sometimes, too, there are conflicts between work time and personal time. Therefore, we have devoted part of this book to personal-time concerns. We show you how to make the best use of your time in all aspects of your life. We all play many different roles, and juggling them becomes an exhaustive time game. We want to help you win this game because it's *the* game that counts.

To make this book more valuable to you, take a few minutes to answer these four questions:

1. What do I wish I had more time for?
2. What would I like to spend less time on?
3. What would I like to have happening in my life that is not happening now?
4. What do I really want from this book?

Voltaire, the great French writer and philosopher, suggested that time enlivens all that is great. Let the greatness of your potential run free. Let the time of your life be all it can be. Take control, and live your life on purpose. Carpe diem! Seize the day!

Two
Focusing on Results

Winners focus, losers spray.

Sidney Harris, syndicated columnist

Chapters 2 through 12 begin with short quizzes. Be sure to take them. In Chapter 13, you'll see how to combine all your chapter quiz scores into a personal Time-Management Profile that indicates your time mastery level.

Before reading this chapter, please circle your response to each of the following statements. A scoring guide is at the end of the chapter.

SA = Strongly Agree MA = Mildly Agree U = Undecided
MD = Mildly Disagree SD = Strongly Disagree

							Score
1.	I write annual performance goals for my job.	SA	MA	U	MD	SD	_____
2.	I keep a master list of all the smaller jobs and assignments that need to be handled over the next several weeks.	SA	MA	U	MD	SD	_____
3.	I review my longer-range goals every day.	SA	MA	U	MD	SD	_____
4.	I constantly ask myself how what I am doing will help me achieve my goals.	SA	MA	U	MD	SD	_____
					Total Score		_____

It is a regular occurrence around this busy office. The general manager is hustling to get some notes together, shouting last-minute instructions to the secretary. The staff looks a little less ambitious but steadily move toward the conference room. After all, planning meetings are important.

The trainees are coming too. They are equipped with shiny new folders, with the company's new insignia stamped in gold on the front. Even their pens display the company's novel emblem.

"What do we do at this meeting?" asks the newest recruit.

"We plan," answers another, with three weeks' seniority. "I'm not sure what we're planning for, but I think the others know."

The young trainee may be surprised to learn that he isn't the only one in the dark at the meeting. In fact, several of the regular planners have only a vague idea of the company's purpose—although they're very reluctant to admit their ignorance after being with the company for one, five, or even ten years. It's amazing how many people not only advocate more planning but spend hours in meetings attempting to plan without knowing their goals. Of course, most people have some vague impressions to work with, but the real goal eludes them. The result is a great deal of wasted time for all concerned.

It is impossible to plan well without knowing your goal. A good example of this point is illustrated in Lewis Carroll's *Alice in Wonderland*. The scene is a fork in the road which Alice has come to on her journey. The Cheshire cat sits high in the tree that stands in the middle of the fork, and a bewildered Alice begins this conversation:

> *Alice:*   Tell me, please, which way I should go from here.
> *Cat:*   That depends on where you want to get to.
> *Alice:*   I don't know for sure where. . . .
> *Cat:*   Then it doesn't matter which road you take.
> *Alice:*   Oh, but I want to get somewhere.
> *Cat:*   You're bound to, if you walk long enough.

Most people live their lives in the same way as Alice does as she walked down that road: They don't know where they're going. They respond and react—or sometimes overreact—to pressures from other people or events. If you want to control your time and increase your effectiveness, you must determine exactly what your goals are and keep them up-to-date. Goals protect you from aimless wandering and point you in a positive direction. Without goals, you are likely to find yourself being swayed by all kinds of outside pressures, first in one direction, then in another. The question you must ask is this: "What is the best use of my time?" The answer requires that you know what your goals are—exactly what results you are trying to achieve.

Understanding the Value of Goals

Goals are the building blocks of better time utilization. In fact, it is impossible to make good use of your time without a set of well-defined goals. How can you evaluate whether one activity represents a better or worse use of your time than another activity if you don't know what the end result of all your activities should be? If you don't have specific goals, it really doesn't matter whether you balance your books, go to a movie, call a friend, or brush your teeth. No matter what you do, the time will pass. One activity is as good as another.

Goals are also an important element in maintaining personal stability. A poignant reminder of this occurred when Buzz Aldrin, one of the first astronauts to reach the moon, suffered an emotional breakdown shortly after his return to earth. To many people, this was a mystery. "Why," they asked, "should this happen to Aldrin, of all people?"

To the outside observer it appeared that Aldrin had everything going his way. And in many ways, he certainly did. He wrote a book about his experiences in which he answered the questions of puzzled observers (Edwin E. Aldrin with Wayne Warga, *Return to Earth*, New York: Random House, 1973). He said the reason for his collapse was simple. "I forgot," he wrote, "that there was life after the moon." He had no other goals once he returned to earth. He found it virtually impossible to function in such a personal vacuum.

Many executives dedicate all their energies to their work, live through the ups and downs of their corporation, and finally retire at age 65 after accomplishing a great deal. Within eighteen months, they are dead. Why? Studies strongly suggest that these executives have much in common with Buzz Aldrin: They have no further goals to live for once they reach the end of their careers. Without goals, they lose their pupose and direction and decide, often unconsciously, that life is no longer worth living.

Maxwell Maltz, author of the best-seller *Psycho-Cybernetics* (New York: Grosset & Dunlap, 1970), put it this way:

> We are engineered as goal seeking mechanisms. We are built that way. When we have no personal goal which we are interested in and means something to us, we have to go around in circles, feel lost, and find life itself aimless and purposeless. We are built to conquer environment, solve problems, achieve goals, and we find no real satisfaction or happiness in life without obstacles to conquer and goals to achieve. People who say that life is not worthwhile are really saying that they themselves have no personal

goals that are worthwhile. Get yourself a goal worth working for. Better still, get yourself a project. Decide what you
want out of a situation. Always have something ahead to
look forward to.

Whether you are concerned with personal time management or
on-the-job time management, *goals* is the key word—the bull's-eye
word, the word you should underline in red. Without goals, time
management is like a hammer without a nail. Without goals, your
efforts lead to nothing. With goals, however, time management becomes a magic key to success, and your goal becomes a possibility
because now you are living your life and working for specific purposes.

Avoid Activity Traps

We often think that people who live in a flurry of activities must get a
lot done. It's not necessarily true. Unfortunately, these people are
often caught in activity traps.

George Odiorne first discussed this idea in his book *Management
and the Activity Trap* (New York: Harper & Row, 1974). According to
Odiorne, we fall into an activity trap when we become so engrossed
in an activity that we lose sight of its purpose. We fall into activity
traps in the absence of goals. When there is no goal to serve as a focal
point, the activity itself takes on the main emphasis. Why? We must
focus on something. If there is no goal, the focus must be on the
activity. Unfortunately, this switching of means and ends is unlikely
to produce the results we want.

There are only two ways to approach time management. You will
either focus primarily on the results you intend to achieve, or you will
focus on the activities you are doing. Of course, there is a relationship
between goals and activities. You can't *do* a goal—you *achieve* it. You
do activities. If you do the right activities, you'll achieve the goal.

Most of our focus, most of the time, is on activities. In part because the goal is not clear; in part because it is what we have learned
to do. But, no matter the reason, there are glaring differences between the two approaches. People who focus primarily on their intended results tend to plan more. They are more proactive, have a
definite action plan, and are usually more productive. They also tend
to have calmer days. People who focus primarily on activities tend to
be more spontaneous and react to whatever happens around them.
They are always busy but not always productive. Their days are usually more chaotic.

Activity traps can occur even in an organization that supposedly manages by objectives or goals. It's interesting to see how this develops. Suppose that you begin writing annual performance goals. We know that whenever goals are written down, the probability of achieving them increases. The result, however, does not happen automatically. You must still take action in order to accomplish the goals. But when do you become concerned about making progress toward the goal?

Focusing More on Your Goals

Most of us tend to wait until a deadline approaches. When you were in school, when did you do your homework? Probably at the last minute. When do you become concerned about accomplishing an annual goal? Toward the end of the year, of course. Becoming concerned toward the end of the year is certainly better than never becoming concerned at all. However, the more frequently you are concerned, the more likely you are to achieve the goal.

Suppose you break down each annual goal into quarterly goals. You will probably become most concerned about accomplishing quarterly goals toward the end of the quarter. But now you are spurred to action four times a year, not just once. If quarterly goals are broken down into monthly goals, you will obviously become concerned about the accomplishment of monthly goals toward the end of each month. But now you are excited twelve times each year. If monthly goals are broken down into weekly goals, you will become excited about the accomplishment of goals fifty-two times each year. And if you can break down weekly goals into daily goals, you will have made long-range goals operational on a daily basis. When will you become concerned about daily goals? Probably toward the latter part of the day. When concern occurs this frequently, results are bound to follow.

Goals should be related to one another. They exist in a hierarchy, as shown in Figure 2-1. The accomplishment of daily goals should lead to the achievement of weekly goals; the accomplishment of weekly goals should lead to the achievement of monthly goals; and so on up to the achievement of long-range goals.

How often should goals be considered? Every day. How far into the future should goals be projected? As far as possible. The further goals are projected into the future, the easier it is to know what to do right now, to sort out the daily details. Personal goals might be projected for a lifetime. On the job, some goals might be projected several years into the future.

Figure 2-1.   The goals pyramid.

Approaching goals in this interlocking fashion is one way of making our habits work for us instead of against us. By habit, most of us put things off until deadlines approach. By breaking goals down into subparts as small as days or weeks, we change the structure of the deadlines. The old habit will work in the same fashion, but this time it will be working for us instead of against us.

Differentiate Between Long- and Short-Range Goals

Most of us have a very short thinking horizon—only a week or two. Even though we are used to writing performance objectives for our jobs, we spend most of our time thinking about what will happen in the next few days or weeks. It isn't that we never think about long-range issues, it's just that we don't do it very often.

One of the best things you can do is to force yourself to review your long-range goals daily. Post them on the wall, if you must. It will help you stay focused and sort out all the trivia that fills your days.

Another problem concerns whether to concentrate on long-range goals or on short-range goals. The two are often in conflict. Of course, writing long-range goals is good, but they don't necessarily guide our daily behavior. We're more likely to pay attention to something else on a day-by-day basis.

Daily behavior is more often controlled by routine tasks and projects. These projects are our short-range goals. Most of us keep a master list of all the jobs and assignments we must take care of over the next several weeks. Completed jobs are crossed off, while new assignments are added to the bottom of the list. After most of the jobs have been crossed off, its hard to review the remaining items. At that point, we write a new list, putting all the leftover items together at the top of a new page. Once again, new assignments are added, and completed ones are crossed off. This is really a perpetual add-scratch-

and-carry list. We call it a Master To-Do List or a Project Summary Record. Figure 2-2 shows a typical example.

Theoretically, the shorter-term projects should all relate to longer-range goals. Right. But how often do they? Whenever we've asked people to compare the two, there is always a gap. Some of the short-term projects don't lead to any of the longer-range goals. How-

Figure 2-2. Project record or master to-do list.

Master To-Do List
Project Summary Record

Priority	Seq	Activity - Description	Due Date	Time Needed	Start Date	

ever, these short-term projects are more likely to control and guide our daily actions.

The point is obvious: The more our short-term goals are in harmony with our long-term goals, the better time managers we'll be. Here are three good ideas that will help you minimize the gap between short-term and long-term goals.

1. *Keep a Master To-Do List.* Be sure to add priority codes. This will show how each entry relates to a long-term goal. Of course, there will still be some projects that don't lead to any long-term goal, but simply by forcing yourself into a priority code system you will be aware of the problem. You can now consider how to drop the item.

2. *Be sure there is a due date assigned to each project.* An approaching deadline creates pressure to get moving. Remember, most of us do not get moving until just before the deadline. Without a due date you never know when the deadline is. However, as the due date gets closer, the pressure to get started builds. Without a deadline, there is no sense of urgency, and the task is more likely to be put off.

3. *Estimate the time required to complete the project.* Knowing the due date and the time you need, you can determine when you must begin. Delay beyond the logical starting point, and you have another last-minute rush job, increased pressure, or an unnecessary crisis.

Write SMART Goals

Preparing well-defined goals is more difficult than most people think. It involves a lot more than writing a glorified "wish list." A good goal is one that motivates you to take action and provides direction for that action. It's more work, but it's worth more, too. To get started, just think SMART: Specific, Measurable, Achievable, Realistic, and Timed. The following criteria will help you improve your efforts and enable you to develop good goals.

1. *Goals should be specific.* When goals are stated in vague terms, they provide very little direction. It is difficult to know exactly where to start and in what direction to proceed. For example, suppose you set this goal: "Increase sales." While this may be an admirable intention, it is not nearly as specific as if you had said: "Increase sales by 10 percent within six months." The latter goal is specific.

2. *Goals should be measurable.* Goals should be quantified whenever possible. This makes it easy to tell if you are making progress. If numbers can't be attached directly to the goal, try using an indirect measurement. When you simply can't quantify goals directly or in-

directly, you will have to make a subjective judgment about your progress. But first see if you cannot restate the goal in such a way that measurement is possible. For example, your initial goal statement might have been, "I want to be rich." Restated better, it might say, "I want to have $3 million in the bank within ten years." You could easily measure progress against the restated version, while it's difficult to measure the original statement.

3. *Goals should be achievable.* Setting a goal is the first step in attaining it. If the goal is unattainable, however, it is not a goal at all. Fantasies, daydreams, aspirations, good intentions, and generalizations won't do. This doesn't mean that you should set your goals low. Goals should make you stretch and grow. They should be challenging, but they must also be achievable. They should be set at a level at which you are both able and willing to work. In general, your motivation increases as you set your goals higher. But if a goal is so high that you don't believe it can be achieved, you will probably never start.

Attainability is difficult to pin down. Ultimately, each person and each organization must judge what is truly attainable. History is filled with examples of people achieving "unattainable" goals. If it feels right to you and if it makes sense to you, then it is probably possible. The danger to avoid is to be so optimistic that you set too many goals to be accomplished in too short a time.

4. *Goals should be realistic.* A realistic goal takes into account available time, resources, and skills. "Achievable" and "realistic" are often related issues. For example, you may be able to complete a project, but not in twelve months. With present resources, you could complete the project in eighteen months. With additional resources, you might complete it in ten months. Either way, it is achievable, but it would be unrealistic as a one-year goal.

5. *Goals should be timed.* Assigning target dates for accomplishing goals increases motivation, commitment, and action. Goals without time schedules quickly become daydreams under the pressure of daily affairs. For each step along the way you should set a realistic target date that can, and should, be adjusted if conditions change. As each target is reached, you gain a sense of accomplishment and greater confidence in your ability to achieve even higher goals.

In addition to the SMART criteria, well-clarified goals have at least three other characteristics.

1. *Goals should be compatible.* Your goals must be compatible with one another. If they are not, accomplishing one goal may prevent you

from accomplishing another. This leads to indecision and uncertainty about which goal to pursue, and you may end up pursuing no goal at all.

2. *Goals should be your own.* You are more likely to work at and accomplish goals that you set for yourself. This doesn't mean you cannot accept a goal that your boss, friend, or spouse wants you to accomplish. But your motivation will be higher if you consciously consider the advantages and disadvantages of the proposed course of action and then make your own decision. You should own at least some part of the goal. You should be willing to listen and talk to others, but you must do your own thinking and deciding. The more the goal is your own, the greater your commitment to its accomplishment.

3. *Goals should be written.* Many of us think that writing goals is unnecessary. We often say that we keep goals in our head, and as long as we think about them it doesn't matter whether or not the goals are written down. This is dangerous reasoning. The purpose of writing goals is to clarify them. There seems to be a special kind of magic in writing goals. Once a goal is written, you have more invested in it than before. As your investment increases, your personal commitment increases.

We all can improve our goals by checking them against these eight criteria. Use a worksheet to list your goals (see Figure 2-3). The more closely the goals match the criteria, the more direction and purpose they will add to your use of time. Remember that writing goals is a skill. Like any skill, it improves with practice.

Focusing on Goals as a Way of Life

Focusing on results must become a habit. Setting goals—and striving to reach them—must become a way of life. Never make a phone call, hold a meeting, or go see someone without first thinking about what you hope to achieve. Continually ask yourself how what you are doing will help you achieve your intended results. When you stop thinking about intended results, you risk falling into activity traps.

To develop the results habit, think about what you are trying to accomplish every year, every month, every week, every day, every hour, every minute. Be sure you have at least one significant goal every day, and don't quit until you reach your daily goals. Before long, you will develop the habit of setting goals and reaching them.

The importance of goals cannot be overemphasized. They are extremely potent. They are powerful because they work. They lead to

Figure 2-3. Goals worksheet.

Longer-Range Goals

Write S.M.A.R.T. goals; be sure they are specific, measurable, achievable, realistic and timed.

GOALS: Results I intend to achieve.

RESULTS: *What I actually achieved.*

accomplishment. Once you begin achieving things that are important to you, you become addicted to achievement. As you reach one level of goals you aim at even higher goals you once considered unattainable.

The alternative? Well, remember the conversation between Alice and the Cheshire cat at the beginning of this chapter? When you don't know where you're going, any road may take you there. And as many people have discovered, when you don't know where you're going, you'll probably wind up somewhere else. If you want to avoid a long, random walk to nowhere, just set some goals and stay focused on them at all times.

	SA	MA	U	MD	SD
Scoring Guide for Chapter Two Quiz					
1.	5	4	3	2	1
2.	5	4	3	2	1
3.	5	4	3	2	1
4.	5	4	3	2	1

Three
Clarifying Priorities

Besides the noble art of getting things done, there is the noble art of leaving things undone. The wisdom of life lies in eliminating the nonessentials.

Chinese proverb

Before reading this chapter, please circle your response to each of the following statements. A scoring guide is at the end of the chapter.

SA = Strongly Agree   MA = Mildly Agree   U = Undecided
MD = Mildly Disagree   SD = Strongly Disagree

Score

1. When I first get to work in the   SA   MA   U   MD   SD   _____
   morning, I usually start the
   day with coffee, conversation,
   or reading the newspaper.

2. I prioritize my various jobs   SA   MA   U   MD   SD   _____
   and activities.

3. I tend to do the quick, easy, or   SA   MA   U   MD   SD   _____
   enjoyable jobs first.

4. Constantly switching priorities   SA   MA   U   MD   SD   _____
   is a big problem on my job.

Total Score   _____

We love fantasies. "The Ugly Duckling" is one of our favorites. What a beautiful story. The poor ugly duckling grew up to be a beautiful, graceful swan. How we wish life were like that. Unfortunately, reality suggests that the ugly duckling grows up to be an ugly duck.

Many of us fantasize about time. We dream of the day when

everything will fit together nicely—when the ugly duckling becomes the beautiful swan. The day when we'll be able to finish everything—on time and without rushing. The day when . . .

Time for a dose of reality: That day will never come. Entropy is a primary force. Left to themselves, things tend to get worse, not better. You will always have more to do, but no more time to do it in. Something will always be left over. The nature of the leftovers is what will determine your success.

Remember George Odiorne's activity trap described in Chapter Two? When you lose sight of your goal, you simply concentrate on activities instead and end up going nowhere. In a related point, Peter Drucker says that many of us seem to be more concerned with doing things right than with doing the right things (Peter F. Drucker, *The Effective Executive*, New York: Harper & Row, 1966). Form over function. Activity traps. But activity traps are avoidable if only we stay focused on the goal. And that's what priorities are all about.

Yes, we're sometimes more concerned with doing things right than with doing the right things. It's very difficult to get good results when you lose sight of the objective. But focusing on the objective isn't enough. We must also sort out all the possible actions and decide which ones to work on first.

Deciding Where to Start

Why do we do what we do when we do it? What criteria do we use for allocating our time? We have many different ways of deciding what we are going to do at any given point during a day. Following are twenty-one of the most common criteria we use to govern our time:

1. We do what we like to do before we do what we don't like to do.
2. We tackle what we know how to do faster than we tackle what we don't know how to do.
3. We do the easy jobs before we do the difficult jobs.
4. We do the quick tasks before we do those that require a lot of time.
5. We do activities we have the resources for.
6. We do things that are scheduled (for example, meetings) before we do nonscheduled things.
7. We sometimes do things that are planned before we do things that are unplanned.

8. We respond to the demands of others before we respond to demands from ourselves.
9. We do jobs that are urgent before we do jobs that are important but not urgent.
10. We readily respond to crises and emergencies.
11. We do activities that are politically expedient or those that advance our personal goals.
12. We wait until a deadline approaches before we really get moving on projects.
13. We do things that are interesting before we do uninteresting things.
14. We do things that provide the most immediate closure.
15. We respond on the basis of who wants it.
16. We respond on the basis of the consequences to us for doing or not doing something.
17. We tackle small jobs before we tackle large jobs.
18. We work on things in the order of their arrival.
19. We work on the basis of the squeaky-wheel principle (the squeaky wheel gets the grease).
20. We work on the basis of consequences to the group.
21. We do things by habit, without thinking about the best sequence.

Most of these criteria represent long-standing habit patterns. We tend to travel the road of least resistance instead of an initially more difficult road that will lead us somewhere. The older we get, the more these habits force us to believe that we can't change, that things must be done in a certain way.

When you seriously think about it, it is not too difficult to determine the best use of your time. You know you ought to do the things that are most important, those valuable activities that contribute to your goals. However, you don't always do it that way. Often, you prefer to work at tasks that you like or find interesting. You do this even though these activities may contribute much less to your goals than the more difficult, complex activities. When you examine yourself, you will probably see several ways in which you allocate time poorly.

Despite what you say is important to you, what you do reflects your true choices and priorities. The several dozen incidents that engage you during the normal day all involve priority decisions. Many of these decisions are made unconsciously. Yet they are made. Whenever you decide, for whatever reason, to engage in one action, you decide against engaging in another action at that point.

A clear understanding of priorities is very important. Most of us agree that priorities concern arranging items in their order of value or importance. The way we should operate is to make sure that the things we do first are the most important things. We should strive to do the most important things now and the less important things later. Personality, emotions, feelings, and attitudes, however, get in the way. Our rational, logically determined priorities often take second place to our gut reactions, preferences, and prejudices.

Most of us have a fuzzy grip on priorities. We use the word *priority* to describe an important project or responsibility connected with our jobs. Under this definition, we would say that a small portion of our time is devoted to priorities. We would be correct in stating that it is simply not possible to always work on the basis of priorities.

The dictionary defines *priority* as something given prior attention—in other words, something done before something else. This definition gets right to the heart of spending time. Everything you do during the day involves a priority decision. Unfortunately, many priority decisions are not made consciously and do not reflect stated goals. Nevertheless, the dozens of priority decisions made each day, consciously or unconsciously, go a long way toward determining what the entire organizational team considers to be important.

Determining What Is Important

Establishing priorities is difficult for many of us. "How," we ask, "can you say one item is more important than another item when everything is important?" We agree that setting priorities can be difficult, but it must still be done. The alternative to consciously setting priorities is unconsciously reacting to demands as they occur. Reacting seldom brings best results. Initiating action requires control coupled with decision-making abilities. Actions initiated on the basis of carefully thought-out decisions are almost always better than actions initiated haphazardly. You may not always establish the best priorities, but your odds are greater with careful thought.

In your efforts to establish priorities, ask yourself the following eight questions:

1. What are my goals? If I had to identify my primary goal, which one would it be?
2. By what criteria do I now establish priorities? (Review the twenty-one points listed at the beginning of this chapter.)
3. How can careful timing and coordination of my goals help me become more effective?
4. Since I feel all my goals are important, how can I make sure

that the activities required for one goal don't hinder another goal?
5. Do I have a good understanding of cause-and-effect relationships on my job? Do I thoroughly understand what activities lead to the results I need? If I don't, where can I get some answers?
6. Which of my goals will bring the greatest value to the company?
7. Which of my goals will bring the greatest personal satisfaction?
8. Which goals are beneficial to the greatest number of people?

Remember, too, that difficult as it is to set priorities, you make a priority decision even when you decide not to set priorities. By default you allow any urgent activity to control your time while items of greater importance go unattended.

Distinguish Between Important and Urgent

During World War II, General Dwight D. Eisenhower used to discuss activities and priorities with his staff. He told his officers that there was an inverse relationship between things that are important and things that are merely urgent. The more important an item, the less likely that it is urgent; the more urgent an item, the less likely that it is important.

Important things are those that contribute significantly to our goals—they have high value. The more direct the contribution, the more important the activity. Important things also tend to have long-term consequences. They make a difference for a long time. Urgent things have short-term consequences. They must be done now; they won't wait. They may or may not relate to our goals. They may or may not make significant contributions. They frequently do not. But urgent things are far more demanding than important things.

We live in constant tension between the urgent and the important. Our problem is that important things seldom must be done today, or even this week. Important things are seldom urgent. Urgent things, however, call for our attention—making endless demands of us, applying pressure every hour, every day.

We seldom question urgent things, never knowing for sure whether they're really urgent or only seemingly so. Sometimes we also develop the habit of responding as if they were urgent when they're not. Indeed, many apparently urgent things only appear to be so. What we need is the widsom, the courage, and the discipline to do the important things first—to break the tyranny of the urgent.

This matrix shown in Figure 3-1 can be a valuable way to analyze your activities and help discover your tendencies. To begin your analysis, think about one cell at a time and consider which parts of your job belong in that cell. Examine each activity in your time log and ask where in the matrix it should be placed.

Cell 1 includes things that are both important and urgent. We tend to call these crises, or problems. Most of us would prefer to see fewer of these activities on a regular basis. Examples include a work strike, conflict with a major customer, a rapidly approaching deadline for submitting next year's budget, or three key people out sick on the same day. Items that fall in Cell 1 tend to be worked on very quickly. In fact, we have very little trouble finding time for items in Cell 1; we simply drop everything and take care of them. If we spend too much time in Cell 1, we practice management by crises.

Cell 2 includes items that are important but not urgent. These are usually opportunities, or high payoff items. This cell, though, is characterized by what isn't happening—or isn't happening often enough. Examples include planning, training, or developing subordinates. Few of us spend as much time in these areas as we ought to. Why? Because they're not urgent. They can be postponed. That's the problem. Important tasks rarely must be done today, or even this week. But the urgent tasks call for constant action, making endless demands, putting pressure on us hour after hour, day after day. Peter Drucker (*The Effective Executive*) observed that we should be just as quick to take care of our opportunities (Cell 2) as we are to take care of our problems (Cell 1). Few of us are. However, even a small increase in Cell 2 usually has a tremendous impact.

Figure 3-1. The important-urgent matrix.

	Important: yes	Important: no
Urgent: yes	Crisis Problem **1**	Routine Interruptions **3**
Urgent: no	**2** Opportunity High Payoff	**4** Trivia Waste

The key to greater results is to spend as much time as possible in Cell-2 activities. Steve Covey (*The Seven Habits of Highly Effective People*, New York: Simon & Schuster, 1989) suggests a question that could help: "If you were to do one thing that you know would have enormously positive results, what would it be?" The answer will probably be one of the things you wish you had more time for (check your responses to the first question at the end of Chapter One). The key to doing these things is to schedule activities related to them. For years, we've noticed that most of us don't regularly schedule activities for the things we wish we had more time for. Covey says that the key is not to prioritize what's on your schedule, but to schedule your priorities.

Events in *Cell 3* consume a large portion of our day. Much of the activity in this cell is spent on the routine and trivial. Because they make up so much of the daily work load, these events may seem more urgent than they really are. They also contribute relatively little to our objectives. Telephone calls are a prime example. If we keep a record of all the phone calls we receive for a period of time, most of us will find that only a small proportion of the calls are really important. Yet all of them take up time. Drop-in visitors are another example. Most drop-in visitors bring relatively unimportant news; only a few bring really important information. Still, it is not unusual for events in Cell 3 to account for 50 to 70 percent of our day.

We like to believe that *Cell 4* does not exist. Items in this block are neither urgent nor important. Yet observation indicates that any where from 10 to 40 percent of our day may be consistently spent on items in Cell 4. Trips to the coffee machine, socializing, long lunch hours, arriving later or leaving early, putting together football pools, and dozens of similar activities are included in Cell 4. Some of the things in Cell 4 are done simply because they are fun or enjoyable or break the monotony of the day.

Every activity has some degree of importance and some degree of urgency. Taking the time and effort to sort out your daily activities into this important-urgent matrix is a worthwhile undertaking. It will, no doubt, show you what percentage of your time is spent on important affairs and what percentage is spent on relatively unimportant issues. It will also indicate to you where you can find additional time to spend on important activities.

As you do this exercise, be as honest with yourself as you can. Most of us believe that virtually everything we do is important. Even if that were true, these things certainly are not all *equally* important. Some things are far more important than others. Even though it may be painful to admit it, we spend much of our day engaged in relatively trivial activities.

While attempting to reallocate activities to gain more value from your time, try to remember Pareto's principle. Vilfredo Pareto, a nineteenth-century scholar, discovered that in any set of elements the critical elements usually constitute a minority of the set. Over the years this concept has evolved into the so-called 80-20 rule: 80 percent of the value comes from 20 percent of the items, whereas the remaining 20 percent of the value comes from 80 percent of the items (see Figure 3-2).

For example, 80 percent of your sales may be made to 20 percent of your customers; 80 percent of your profit may come from 20 percent of your product line; 80 percent of your problems may come from 20 percent of your employees. You might even say that 80 percent of the results you achieve are accounted for by 20 percent of the things you do. What are your critical 20 percent of activities?

This 80-20 rule can be related to the Important-Urgent matrix. Items that fall into Cell 2 (important but not urgent) are usually part of the 20 percent that contribute 80 percent to your results. This was illustrated for us recently when a friend of ours suffered a heart attack and was forced to stay home for six months. At first, he was able to return to work only for three or four hours a day. Yet he discovered that he could achieve virtually the same results in three or four hours as he had previously achieved in eight or nine hours. How was he able to do this? Realizing that he would have only a few hours to accomplish anything, he decided to spend those hours on only the most important activities.

The secret is simply to stop doing some of the unimportant things and begin doing more of the important things. A group of stockbrokers learned this lesson and raised their income in the process. After examining their client records carefully, they discovered that 79 percent of their total income was derived from 13 percent of their clientele. At the same time, they realized that they spent very little time on that 13 percent segment. By rearranging their tasks so

Figure 3-2.   The 80-20 rule.

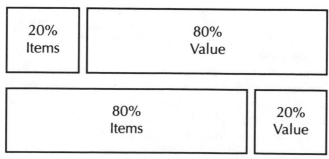

that they spent more time with their high-value group, they rapidly increased their total volume of business. It seems that these clients were also using other brokers. As the stockbrokers spent more time with these high-value clients, they began to receive an even greater percentage of the clients' total business.

If you analyze things in terms of the 80-20 rule, you will soon discover that virtually 80 pecent of everything you do is low in value. If you are spending 80 percent of your time on these activities, you are not managing your time wisely. Learn to focus your time on the things that really count.

Defining Personal and Professional Goals

The priority, or value, of an activity is measured by its contribution to a goal. Those activities that lead directly to goal achievement are the most important. The question, though, is which goal, or perhaps *whose* goal? Most of us come to work with personal goals as well as organizational goals. Important activities are those leading to either organizational goals or to personal goals. When conflicts arise between personal and organizational goals, personal goals tend to take precedence. In some cases people pursue personal goals to the detriment of organizational goals. Just because we're at work doesn't mean we're working.

How do organizational and personal goals differ? Organizational goals are carefully and logically determined. Frequently we must discuss them with other people in order to define them exactly. An organizational goal is one that we understand and commit to intellectually. A personal goal, on the other hand, is a private and often purely emotional commitment. It need not make sense to anyone except us. No one else may even know what it is. But we have committed ourselves to it on an emotional level.

A conflict between organizational and personal goals is a conflict between an intellectual commitment and an emotional commitment. The emotional commitment is the one that usually prevails, other things being equal. In the event of truly significant conflict, emotional choice comes out on top every time.

The conflict between personal and professional goals is dramatically illustrated in a recent study (Fred Luthans, Richard M. Hodgetts, and Stuart A. Rosenkrantz, *Real Managers*, Cambridge, Mass.: Ballinger, 1988). Researchers asked several hundred managers about how they spend their time. Their intent was to show how much time was spent in different parts of the manager's job. Managers were also classified on the basis of success and effectiveness. Success was measured by how fast the manager was being promoted. Effectiveness was measured by how well the manager achieved company goals. Figure 3-3 shows the results of the study.

Most managers apparently choose between effectiveness and success. Only 8 percent of the managers sampled measured high on both scales. Depending on their choice, they will also spend their time in very different ways. Networking is something to be considered very carefully. Although it is very important for success, it is much less important for effectiveness. However, we suspect that any time spent networking is very easy to rationalize. Above all, we must be clear on what we choose to pursue—and why.

Some managers are more interested in personal promotion than in corporate results. Some managers are more interested in lording it over others than in being truly effective managers. They define management as gaining status, not serving others. Some mangers act more from ego, selfishness, and paranoia than to seek the best interests of employees or company. Unfortunately, some managers don't

Figure 3-3.   How managers spend their time.

Time Spent On	Successful Managers	Effective Managers	Successful and Effective Managers
Traditional Management Functions Planning, organizing, making decisions, controlling	13%	19%	32%
Human Resources Management Motivating, reinforcing, staffing, managing conflict, training and developing, disciplining	11%	26%	20%
Routine Communication Exchanging information and handling paperwork	28%	44%	29%
Networking Interacting with outsiders, socializing, politicking	48%	11%	19%

Source: Fred Luthans, Richard M. Hodgetts, and Stuart A. Rosenkrantz, *Real Managers* (Cambridge, Mass.: Ballinger, 1988).

even realize what they are doing. The General Bullmoose syndrome obscures their vision; they assume that whatever is good for them must automatically be good for the company.

Some conflict between personal and corporate objectives is inevitable. To the extent that you can avoid it, your life becomes much simpler. To the extent that you cannot avoid it, you must come to grips with your own set of values and your sense of right and wrong.

Setting priorities means deciding what to do first. We pick our priorities both consciously and unconsciously. Remember, you never have time to do everything, but you do have enough time for what's most important—if you choose wisely. How you arrange your priorities has much to do with the results you ultimately achieve.

Scoring Guide for Chapter Three Quiz					
	SA	MA	U	MD	SD
1.	1	2	3	4	5
2.	5	4	3	2	1
3.	1	2	3	4	5
4.	1	2	3	4	5

Four
Analyzing Time

Nothing is easier than being busy, and nothing more difficult than being effective.

Alec MacKenzie,
The Time Trap

Before reading this chapter, please circle your response to each of the following statements. A scoring guide is at the end of the chapter.

SA = Strongly Agree   MA = Mildly Agree   U = Undecided
MD = Mildly Disagree   SD = Strongly Disagree

Score

1. At least once a year, I keep a   SA   MA   U   MD   SD   _____
record of how I actually spend
my time for a week or two.

2. I constantly analyze   SA   MA   U   MD   SD   _____
everything I am doing and
look for ways to improve my
performance.

3. I often have to come in early,   SA   MA   U   MD   SD   _____
stay late, or take work home to
get all my work done.

4. Constantly recurring crises   SA   MA   U   MD   SD   _____
take up too much of my time.

Total Score   _____

What were you doing last Thursday afternoon? Do you remember? How much of your time do you spend answering mail? How many times a day are you interrupted? How much time last week did you spend doing work that really didn't need to be done?

If you're like most people, you *think* you know more about how you spend your time than you actually do. We really believe our memories are "good enough" for an accurate account of the hours and minutes we spend on a given task. However, time after time, we come up short when put to the test.

Here's the truth: We cannot make any significant time improvements until we really know how we spend our time. Would you expect a doctor to prescribe a cure without diagnosing the problem? The same thing holds for you, too. You can't prescribe good time cures without diagnosing time problems.

Most of us incorrectly perceive the nature of our time problems because we fail to analyze our time. Things simply are not the way we think they are. We have often asked people to describe their job as they think it is—to make a list of what they believe they do and how much time they spend doing it. When they compare the list with an actual record of what they do, they're usually surprised at the large differences that appear. Sherlock Holmes often chided Dr. Watson by saying, "Watson, you see, but you do not observe." A similar admonition could easily be applied to most of us. We are so accustomed to doing the things we do, day in and day out, that we act without thinking—and without knowing either.

Habitual behavior consumes a great deal of our time. This behavior is often unconscious. Although we may claim to remember where our times goes, countless studies have demonstrated that we often have no idea of what is happening. Furthermore, because we fail to perceive time use accurately, we frequently think of it as beyond our control. No doubt some of it is beyond our control, but there is still much we can do with the rest of it.

Before we can control our time, though, we must understand how it is truly being used. We must accept the fact that we are the cause of most of our time problems, no matter how much we would like to blame others. We must also acknowledge that the solutions to many of our time problems must come from inside ourselves, not from external sources.

One effective way to analyze your time is to ask a simple but powerful question. As you go through your day, ask yourself, "How is what I am doing right now helping me achieve my objectives?" The more you ask this question, the more you will realize how much irrelevant "stuff" fills your life. Soon, you may become uncomfortable enough to clear some of it out of the way.

Because all of us have so many time problems, it is important to analyze time. No problem can be solved until it is well defined. Quite often, if we try to solve the problem as we think it is, we end up solving the wrong problem, or we make the existing problem worse. Good information about time use leads to good problem definition, which leads to good solutions. Sometimes a careful time analysis will even reveal that the problem is not nearly as serious as we believed.

In order to analyze how we currently use our time, we must collect data. This is the medicine part of the analysis many people wish to avoid, so they just don't do it. Then, of course, they can't hope to get well. There is a price to pay for improved time management, but it's worth it for those who put in the effort. This chapter will help you. It will describe several approaches to collecting data that can be used to gain insight into your present time habits.

Figuring Out the Cost of Your Time

Most of us respond to money, so the dollar value of time is a good place to begin an analysis. In other words, how much are you worth? What is the monetary cost of your time to your organization? Many people have never considered the true cost of their time. For those who want to manage their time more effectively, an understanding of what their time is worth will be valuable.

The following exercise will enable you to calculate your actual cost to your organization. Your cost is based on your salary plus all the other costs of keeping you employed. For example, this exercise assumes that you are neither underpaid nor overpaid but are being paid in direct proportion to what you contribute to your organization.

Before you start, make a guess. Think for a moment about how much you cost your organization. What would you say it costs your employer for one minute of your time? Make a note of your estimated worth. Now, here's how to get the facts.

		You	Example
1. *Annual salary.*		1 _____	$40,000
2. *Fringe benefits.* According to the U.S. Chamber of Commerce, fringe benefits average between 30 and 39 percent of salary costs. If you don't know the exact percent for your organization, use 30 percent.		2 _____	12,000
3. *Total salary plus fringe benefits.*		3 _____	$52,000
4. *Overhead*—office space, furniture, telephone, electricity, heat, air			

	You	*Example*

conditioning, office machines, cafeterias, building maintenance, office supplies, and so on. For larger organizations, overhead will vary from 75 to 100 percent of payroll and fringes. For smaller organizations, overhead may vary from 50 to 75 percent of payroll plus fringes. Unless you know the exact percentage for your organization, use 100 percent of the figure in line 3.

4 _____   52,000

5. *Other expenses*—conferences, meetings, company-related travel, educational reimbursement, professional development, entertainment, or other activities reimbursed by your organization.

5 _____   3,000

6. *Subtotal.* Add lines 3, 4, and 5. This is your cost to the organization at break-even.

6 _____ $107,000

7. *Profit and taxes.* If your organization expects to make a profit, you need to add in your proportion of the profit. Use a figure equal to twice the profit percentage to allow for taxes. For instance, if your firm expects a 10 percent after-tax profit, use 20 percent of the figure shown in line 6.

7 _____   21,400

8. *Total.* Add lines 6 and 7. This is your annual cost to your organization.

8 _____ $128,400

9. *Cost per day.* Divide the figure in line 8 by the number of days you work per year. Most people work about 230 days a year. This assumes 52 weekends, 10 holidays, 10 vacations days, and 10 sick days or personal leave days. If you take a three-week vacation, then you have 225 working days. A four-week vacation would give you 220 working days. On the other hand, a one-week

	You	Example
vacation would leave you 235 working days.	9 _____	$558

10. *Cost per hour.* Divide the figure in line 9 by the number of hours you normally work in a day. This shows your hourly cost to the organization. Place that amount in line 10a. (Eight hours are used in the example.) Some prefer to divide not by the number of total hours on the job but by the number of productive hours on the job. To arrive at productive hours, you need to deduct time for coffee, socializing, waiting, and other nonproductive activities that you engage in each day. Most office personnel report that their productive hours are about 50 to 60 percent of their total hours. Find the cost of productive time by dividing the figure in line 9 by the number of productive hours in your normal day. Place that amount in line 10b. (Five hours are used in the example.)

	You	Example
	10a _____	$70
	10b _____	$112

11. *Cost per minute.* Divide the hourly figure from line 10a or 10b by 60 to find the cost for each minute of your time.

	You	Example
	11a _____	$1.17
	11b _____	$1.87

Does your total cost surprise you? Is it higher than you thought it would be? Most of us underestimate our true cost. Note that in our example, the actual cost is over three times the salary. Most of us will find that—at a minimum—our true cost is at least two to three times our salary.

Now that you know how much your time is worth, you can use this information in several ways. For instance, you could calculate the total cost of a meeting to decide if it's really worth holding. You could use the money value of time to evaluate alternative uses for your time.

You may not consider the waste of a few minutes here and there to be really serious, but think a moment. If you saw a five-dollar bill on the floor, would you pick it up or ignore it? Wasting five minutes could be worth several times as much, yet you would probably feel worse about the loss of the five-dollar bill. Think of time as money. You'll learn to internalize its value beause, as the cliché says, "Money talks!"—and rather loudly, too.

Keeping Track of Your Time

Your time is obviously important, not only to you but to your organization. Keeping a daily time log can help you discover how your time is used. Many people resist the suggestion to keep a time log. A common response is, "I've already got too much to do, and now you want me to keep a written record of how I spend my time? You've got to be kidding!" Besides, they think they really *do* know where their time goes, so a time log would be a useless exercise.

We disagree. From talking to thousands of people about how they use their time, we know that people's memories are not that accurate. We also know that almost everyone who has kept a time log has been rewarded for the effort. People gain valuable insights into their hour expenditures, and they always uncover surprises.

The Diary Time Log

The most common format for a time log is an abbreviated diary, as shown in Figure 4-1. Use it to record everything you do, when you do it, and how long it takes. Begin your record in the morning. Enter your name, the day, and the date at the top. If you place the log on a clipboard, you can carry it with you as you go about the day. Keeping the log in front of you will remind you to keep recording.

Record your time in fifteen-minute segments. During some segments you will be doing only one thing—for instance, attending a meeting. During others, you may be doing several things—for instance, answering two telephone calls, opening your mail, and instructing your secretary. Do not be concerned about capturing every event. Concentrate on the most important ones or the ones that take the longest. You will get enough detail to provide an accurate profile.

Record your activities as you do them, not all at once at the end of the day. Nobody's memory is that good. Resist the tendency to generalize or to make yourself look good on paper. You will only be fooling yourself, and the time invested in the analysis will be wasted. Be as detailed as possible in your recording. Use abbreviations or codes if it is convenient, and make a note of what the codes mean. For instance:

Figure 4-1.   Diary time log.

Time Log Record

Time	Activity - Description	IMP	URG	Interruptions		
				T	V	Description

9:45:   TG dropped in to socialize.
1:20:   FM called about cost report.
2:30:   Dictated letters to BS, LR, and RT.
3:15:   Coffee.

As you record each activity, note both its importance and its urgency. We suggest a simple code—High, Medium, or Low. Impor-

tance always depends on what you are trying to accomplish. The "importance" column should provide an overall picture of your effectiveness in using your time. Urgency is relative to time; as the deadline approaches, urgency increases. The urgency column will give you an idea of the deadline pressures you face.

Record interruptions in the columns provided. Indicate whether the interruptions were from incoming telephone calls or from some other source. Briefly note the nature of the interruption and who was involved. Record outgoing telephone calls as an activity. The recording activity will take a little effort at first, but you will soon get the hang of it. By the third day it will start feeling like part of your regular routine, and it will seem much easier to do. You'll soon see the value for yourself, and you'll be encouraged to keep going.

How long should you record your time? There is no standard answer for this question. You should record your time until you believe you have covered a representative period. For some, this may be two or three days. For others, it may be several weeks or even a month. Most people record one or two weeks.

You should record a time log at least once a year. Furthermore, whenever significant changes occur in your job, you should record a new time log. New conditions may require changes in job habits. A time log is the single best technique for gaining information necessary to make intelligent changes. In general, you should record a time log whenever you want more information about your job.

Remember when you record your time to consider cycles and seasonal changes in your job. Your time record should cover a representative period so you can rely on the data. If your job is highly seasonal you may need two time logs—one for high season and another for low season. This may be true for cyclical swings throughout the year too.

The Matrix Time Log

Another time-log format is what we call the Matrix Log, as shown in Figure 4-2. Activity categories appear at the top of each column. Each row represents a fifteen-minute increment. Every fifteen minutes, you simply check the box that matches your major activity for that time segment.

The advantages of a Matrix Log are simplicity and speed. The disadvantage is the loss of detail. For example, the Matrix Log reflects only the amount of time in a category, wheras the Diary Log provides more detailed information about the activity.

To use the Matrix Log, first decide on the categories for each col-

Figure 4-2.   Matrix time log.

Matrix Time Log

ACTIVITIES / TIME																										
9:00-9:15																										
9:15-9:30																										
9:30-9:45																										
9:45-10:00																										
10:00-10:15																										
10:15-10:30																										
10:30-10:45																										
10:45-11:00																										
11:00-11:15																										
11:15-11:30																										
11:30-11:45																										
11:45-12:00																										
12:00-12:15																										
12:15-12:30																										
12:30-12:45																										
12:45-1:00																										
1:00-1:15																										
1:15-1:30																										
1:30-1:45																										
1:45-2:00																										
2:00-2:15																										
2:15-2:30																										
2:30-2:45																										
2:45-3:00																										
3:00-3:15																										
3:30-3:45																										
3:45-4:00																										
4:00-4:15																										
4:15-4:30																										
4:30-4:45																										
4:45-5:00																										
TOTALS																										

umn. Figure 4-3 is an example of a Matrix Log we have often used with salespeople. Notice that there are two levels of information: (1) what was done, and (2) which account it was done for. Some people even add columns to indicate emotional state or energy level (e.g., how they felt at the time). This kind of information can also be tracked

Figure 4-3. Matrix time log for salespeople.

Sales-Time Log

TIME	CODE			ACCOUNT NAME	FIELD TIME									TRAVEL TIME	ADMIN TIME				PERSONAL TIME
	Customer		Prospect		Selling	Demonstration	Touring	Servicing	Problems	Training	Waiting	Gen. Contact	Prospecting		Planning	Preparation	Paperwork	Problems	
7:00- 7:15																			
7:15- 7:30																			
7:30- 7:45																			
7:45- 8:00																			
8:00- 8:15																			
8:15- 8:30																			
8:30- 8:45																			
8:45- 9:00																			
9:00- 9:15																			
9:15- 9:30																			
9:30- 9:45																			
9:45-10:00																			
10:00-10:15																			
10:15-10:30																			
10:30-10:45																			
10:45-11:00																			
11:00-11:15																			
11:15-11:30																			
11:30-11:45																			
11:45-12:00																			
12:00-12:15																			
12:15-12:30																			
12:30-12:45																			
12:45- 1:00																			
1:00- 1:15																			
1:15- 1:30																			
1:30- 1:45																			
1:45- 2:00																			
2:00- 2:15																			
2:15- 2:30																			
2:30- 2:45																			
2:45- 3:00																			
3:00- 3:15																			
3:15- 3:30																			
3:30- 3:45																			
3:45- 4:00																			
4:00- 4:15																			
4:15- 4:30																			
4:30- 4:45																			
4:45- 5:00																			
5:00- 5:15																			
5:15- 5:30																			
5:30- 5:45																			
5:45- 6:00																			
6:00- 6:15																			
6:15- 6:30																			
6:30- 6:45																			
6:45- 7:00																			
Number of Checkmarks																			

with the Diary Log. At the end of each day, add up the check marks in each column. You can then calculate the hours and the percentage of your time spent in each category.

Have Somebody Log Your Time for You

Instead of recording the log yourself, you might be lucky enough to get some help. You might have an observer follow you around during the day and record what you do. You could use a business student or a trainee at your company. Some companies have methods-improvement departments that can help you. The advantage of having someone else do your time log is that the other person is much more likely to be objective and accurate in recording your activities and the time spent on them. An impartial observer won't forget to record things even though your day gets hectic.

The disadvantages, of course, are that the observer may not be around often enough to capture the variety of activities that fill your days. Also, at times the need for privacy may prevent the outside observer from being present to record what is happening. Furthermore, outside observers cost more than doing it yourself. Unquestionably, there are trade-offs to be considered in deciding whether to record time yourself or have an observer record it for you.

Another alternative—a variation of the observer approach—is to have someone check on your activities at random intervals throughout the day. Or, you could even do random sampling yourself. If you use the random-sampling technique, it will take approximately twenty to thirty observations per day for four to six weeks to provide an accurate profile of your weekly time-use patterns. These observations can be done in person or by telephone.

The Electronic Time Log

Still another option might be to use electronic devices. One example is The Timelogger (Dantronics, Inc., P.O. Box 120678, St. Paul, MN 55112—Tel. 612-484-2108). By simply pressing various keys, you can track your time over a variety of preset categories. According to the manufacturer, using the Timelogger has enabled professionals to increase their billable time by about 13 percent. That's certainly something to think about. We've used the Timelogger ourselves and agree that it's an excellent way to log time.

Most people, of course, do their own time log, using a form similar to ours or a form provided by their organization.

The Special Time Log

In addition to regular time logs, there are several special logs that may prove useful. These include a Telephone Log and an Interruption Log. Examples are shown in Figure 4-4. These specialized logs provide more detailed information than is possible with a regular time log.

Figure 4-4. Interruption log and telephone log.

Date	Time Called	Person Calling	Purpose of Call Topics Discussed	Follow-Up

Telephone Log

T	V	Who	Purpose - Topics Discussed	Beg Time	End Time	Total Time

Interruption Record

Study Time-Log Data

When you have completed your daily time log, the fun begins. Now you get to see what's really happening in your life. Begin by summarizing your day. Then, study the results. The following twelve questions will help you analyze the information from your time log:

1. What went right today? What went wrong? Why?
2. What time did I start my top-priority task? Why? Could I have started earlier in the day?
3. What patterns and habits are apparent from my time log?
4. Did I spend the first hour of my day doing important work?
5. What was the most productive period of my day? Why?
6. What was the least productive period of my day? Why?
7. Who or what caused most interruptions?
8. How might I eliminate or reduce the three biggest time wasters?
9. How much of my time was spent on high-value activity and how much on low-value tasks?
10. What activities could I spend less time on and still obtain acceptable results?
11. What activities needed more time today?
12. What activities could have been delegated? To whom?

As you analyze your time log, look for patterns and trends. How much of your time do you control yourself? How much is controlled by your boss? How much is controlled by the system you work in? How much can you influence boss-controlled or system-controlled time?

Be sure to consider the question of quality time versus quantity time. Quantity is easily measured by the passing of time. Quality is much more difficult. It is not only a function of the amount of time you spend but also of whom you spend it with and of what you spend it on.

Remember that the purpose of any time log is to help you study your activities. Important activities are those that will help you accomplish your goals. A time log is ideally suited to uncovering the activities that simply do not lead to goals. As you record your activities, try to match each activity to a goal. If you discover activities that do not relate to your goals, think about how you can modify, eliminate, or replace them with activities that will help you achieve the results you desire.

You can also use your time log to answer the question, "Who controls my time?" Go through each activity listed and ask yourself whether it represents discretionary time or time controlled by someone else. Caution must be exercised here. It is often easy to assert that someone else is in control of your time when actually you have wide discretion in performing an activity.

As you analyze your time log, you are certain to receive some surprises. You may discover that you are quite a different time manager from what you thought you were. You may be better in some ways and not so good in other ways. You may discover that you are wasting time in ways that you never realized. You will probably be amazed at how much time you spend in some areas and at how little time you spend in other areas. All this information will help you verify exactly how you spend your time so you can make decisions about how to use it better.

Analyzing Your Work

Another valuable exercise is to analyze your job from three different perspectives: (1) what you think you are doing, (2) what you ought to be doing, and (3) what you are actually doing. Examining all three points of view will give you valuable insight into your job and time problems. With this insight you will be able to make decisions about your overall time strategies. In order to bring the three views of your job closer together, you should complete a worksheet like the one illustrated in Figure 4-5.

The Analysis Form

Begin the analysis by writing a brief description of what your job includes—what functions you perform in a typical week. Use the "Priority" column to indicate how much each function contributes to the objectives you are trying to achieve in your job. The more important the functions, the higher the priority value. Then, estimate what percentage of your time is spent in each functional area during the week. If you capture all your job functions, this column should total 100 percent.

Next, consider what isn't happening in your job. There are probably some things you ought to be doing that you are not doing at all. If so, enter those items and show their appropriate priority value. Then record a zero in the "Estimated Time" column to indicate that you aren't spending any time on those items at present.

Now look over all the things you have listed. Consider what percentage of your time you should spend on each item during the week.

Figure 4-5. Subordinate's version of job-work analysis worksheet.

Job-Work Analysis
SUBORDINATE WORKSHEET

Name				Date
JOB FUNCTIONS OR ACTIVITIES	PRIORITY	ESTIMATED TIME	IDEAL TIME	ACTUAL TIME
Briefly describe your job. List the primary parts of your job	Rank order items on the basis of their overall importance	List the percentage of your time you think you now spend on each part of your job.	What percentage of your time do you think you should be spending on each part of your job?	Keep a time log and record how much time you really spend on each part of your job.
TOTALS	XXXXX	100%	100%	100%

If you could really organize your job the way it ought to be, what would it look like? What would be the best way to allocate your time across the various functions so that each function received an appropriate amount? Record these ideal times in the third column. This column should also total 100 percent.

In order to complete the last column, you will need to record your actual time use for a few weeks. Use one of the time logs described earlier. Summarize your time logs and place the results in the last column, labeled "Actual Time."

Analyzing Your Job Yourself

You are now ready to analyze the differences, or variances, between what you think you are doing, what you ought to be doing, and what you are actually doing. You may find you are spending too much time in some parts of your job and too little time in other parts. As you study the variances, you will be in a better position to make the decisions necessary to take charge of your time and your job. You will know what you must do to make your time investment yield a better return. The key is to balance your time by spending the appropriate amount of time for each part.

In order to analyze your job properly, you will have to break it down into meaningful parts. For instance, should you list all your meetings together, regardless of their content, or should you divide them by type? Whatever you are doing on your job, you should break things into as many categories as necessary for the analysis to make sense to you. Don't become overly concerned with classification or other details, however. Even an imperfect analysis will be valuable. Many people find that this technique pinpoints their time problems better than any other approach they have tried.

One other point needs to be considered. Since you are spending all your time now, you must subtract before you can add. If you want to spend more time in one area, you will have to reduce the time in some other area. The adding and subtracting sometimes cross the boundary between work and personal time. All too often hours are subtracted from personal time so they can be added to work time. When this happens, you may pay a greater price than you intended.

Asking Your Boss to Analyze Your Job

You will also find it valuable to compare how you and your superior view your job. Ask your superior to list what he or she believes your job functions are (see Figure 4-6). Also, ask your superior to indicate the priority value and the ideal time allocations.

Superiors and subordinates seldom agree on everything. In fact, we've never seen complete agreement. However, the comparison will point out areas that need discussion. These differences may help explain difficulties like coordinating priorities and activities or why

Figure 4-6.   Superior's version of job-work analysis worksheet.

Job-Work Analysis
SUPERIOR WORKSHEET

Subordinate's Name			Date
JOB FUNCTIONS OR ACTIVITIES	PRIORITY	IDEAL TIME	DIFFERENCES TO DISCUSS
Briefly describe the subordinate's job. List the primary parts of your job	Rank order items on the basis of their overall importance	What percentage of your time do you think you should be spending on each part of your job?	
TOTALS	XXXXX	100%	

some jobs get pushed back more often. At the very least, this exercise will help you and your superior develop a better working consensus of the best way to spend your time.

This job-work analysis may be just the tool you need to encourage better communication between you and your superior about real job expectations. It could help you do a much better job with a lot less effort and get more positive evaluations along the way. Some find that this analysis creates a new job for them—one they enjoy much more.

Many people question the value of a job-function analysis. Why is it necessary? Any time analysis is done for only one reason: to discover the discrepancy between objectives and activities. Although establishing goals is probably the single most important aspect of good time management, you cannot *do* a goal. A goal is an end result, something that is accomplished. You must do activities. If you do the right activities, you have a good chance of reaching your goals. If you do the wrong activities, you may never reach your goals. Activities bridge the gap between where you are now and where you want to be.

Many analyses have revealed that people engage in activities that do not relate to their goals. Without some form of analysis, discrepancies between activities and goals may never come to light. These discrepancies are not necessarily intentional; they're simply the way things develop.

Getting a Return on Time Invested

The Japanese word *kaizen* effectively sums up the rationale for analyzing time. *Kaizen* means continual incremental improvement. Whatever our time habits are, we didn't get that way overnight. We won't change everything overnight, either. The important point, though, is that we can change. By continually looking, you will find more and more ways to improve. That's the whole point of analyzing your time.

From a business standpoint, we want to maximize the return on time invested. The techniques discussed in this chapter will help you determine the value of your present return. The following chapters will focus on how to increase that return.

As we proceed, the value of a single minute will become more and more apparent. A minute is a most revealing time unit. It is so often ignored or dismissed as unimportant. We ask others, unthinkingly, to "give us a minute." We eagerly engage in even the most useless activity because "it only takes a minute." We give little thought to being "a few minutes late." Yet minutes are all we have. A new respect for this small time unit might help us become more successful. The way we put our minutes together determines whether we achieve positive or negative results. It is by putting minutes together that our lifetime is made—or lost.

Scoring Guide for Chapter Four Quiz				
SA	**MA**	**U**	**MD**	**SD**
1.	5	4	3	2	1
2.	5	4	3	2	1
3.	1	2	3	4	5
4.	1	2	3	4	5

Five
Planning Work
and Time

You can't no more do what you ain't prepared for than you can come back from where you ain't been.

Robert Henry

Before reading this chapter, please circle your response to each of the following statements. A scoring guide is at the end of the chapter.

SA = Strongly Agree   MA = Mildly Agree   U = Undecided
MD = Mildly Disagree   SD = Strongly Disagree

							Score
1.	I write out a to-do list every day.	SA	MA	U	MD	SD	_____
2.	I write out a weekly plan, which includes specific goals, activities, priorities, and time estimates for each activity.	SA	MA	U	MD	SD	_____
3.	At least once a week, I meet with others to coordinate plans, priorities, and activities.	SA	MA	U	MD	SD	_____
4.	I often think I should get better organized.	SA	MA	U	MD	SD	_____

Total Score _____

Few of us spend as much time on planning as we know we should, even though planning is crucial to using our time effectively. Planning becomes increasingly important as we move up the executive ladder, because with position come responsibilities for long-range goals. For middle, upper-middle, and top-level managers, it is virtually impossible to achieve carefully determined goals without planning.

Because we fail to plan as we should, we are constantly bumping into Murphy's laws:

1. Nothing is as simple as it seems.
2. Everything takes longer than it should.
3. If anything can go wrong, it will.

However, those of us who spend an adequate amount of time planning run into these problems less often than those who fail to plan.

Understanding the Importance of Planning

Most of us agree that proper planning is vitally important. Why, then, do we not give more time to this important function? Ironically, many of us simply don't have enough time to plan. There are too many other jobs that must be done, and planning can wait for another day. In other words, planning may be important, but it is usually not urgent. Yet if we took more time to plan, we would gain more time for our other job functions as well.

Most of us are very action-oriented. We prefer to be in the thick of battle, doing instead of thinking. As a result, we adopt a reactive pattern. We react to whatever happens around us. Reacting requires very little prior thinking. Proacting, on the other hand, requires a great deal of prior thought and planning. This is difficult to do in a reactively patterned day. Therefore, most of us continue to react rather than carefully plan as many things as we could.

Some people pride themselves on being spontaneous. There seems to be a special virtue attached to spontaneity and a feeling that if we plan carefully, we will miss the important things in life. This, of course, is nonsense. Life is too complex to "wing it" all the time. If you want things to happen right, you must plan at some point. If your time is to be spent well, it must be planned. The better you plan, the more time you will have for taking advantage of opportunities as they arise.

Another problem is that in the past most of us have been reasonably successful without much planning. The business climate was positive and reasonably predictable. Some of us even surpassed our goals. Clearly, it was possible to do well in spite of poor planning. Whether or not we could have been more successful if we had done more planning is a moot point.

Some people have developed a mental block about planning. They view it as a complex, time-consuming activity. The task of planning becomes so enormous in their minds that they are unable to take the first step. Planning need not be a complex undertaking. It simply means thinking about the future in some systematic way. It requires thinking about the events that should be happening and the conditions required to meet these goals.

Planning helps bridge the gap between where you are now and where you hope to be at some future point. Where you are now is one side of the chasm, and your goals are the other side. Unless there is some way to bridge this separation, you will never be able to reach your goals.

Planning is the way we connect future points with today. It has often been noted that the further into the future we can project our goals, the easier it is to know what to do today. However, that future point does not have to be very far off in order to be of benefit.

Winston Churchill once complained, "One must always look ahead, but it is difficult to look farther than one can see." It is only when we have a purpose for tomorrow that today has substance — whether we are talking about the future of a country or the direction of an individual life. Most people think one to two weeks in advance for most of the things that engage their time. Even a one-week time horizon can be extremely valuable.

A $25,000 Idea

When Charles Schwab was president of Bethlehem Steel, he paid $25,000 for one simple idea. That was way back when a dollar was really worth something.

Why pay so much for one idea? Even Schwab's friends questioned his judgment. But Schwab said it was worth it because it was the most profitable lesson he had ever learned. He even said that this one idea helped him turn Bethlehem Steel into the world's largest independent steel producer, earned him over $100 million dollars personally, and made him the best-known steel man in the world.

So what was this fantastic idea? When Schwab asked how to get more done with his time, his consultant said this: "Write down the most important tasks you have to do tomorrow and number them in the order of their importance. When you arrive in the morning, begin at once on number 1 and stay on it until it is completed. Recheck your priorities; then begin with number 2. If any task takes all day, never mind. Stick with it as long as it is the most important one. If you don't finish them all, you probably couldn't do so with any other method, and without some system you would probably not even decide which one was the most important. Make this a habit every working day. When it works for you, teach it to others. Try it as long as you like. Then send me a check for what you think it is worth."

Several weeks later, Schwab sent his check for $25,000 to the consultant. And, from that beginning, the ordinary to-do list has grown to be the most common planning tool in America.

Maintenance vs. Development Work

We all face two kinds of work. On the one hand there are all the jobs that must be done to keep the organization functioning. We call this maintenance work. We are maintaining the current level of operations, getting the work out the door, doing all the housekeeping. On the other hand, there are jobs that must be done to develop the organization. We call this development work. These are things that are not currently happening. We must make room for them somewhere in the schedule.

Maintenance means taking care of present customers; development means finding new customers. Maintenance means keeping the work moving; development means cutting operating costs. Maintenance means continuing present systems; development means improving the systems.

The matrix in Figure 5-1 shows both types of work and the way the work arrives. Activities are either expected or unexpected. The daily routine is expected; the interruptions, problems, and crises are unexpected, even though they happen all the time! Expected work can be planned; unexpected work can only be anticipated or allowed for. Work on our long-range goals is expected; good luck and new opportunities are unexpected.

Because it's part of the daily routine, maintenance work is much more likely to happen. We manage to get the work out today, even though we may never have time to start those improvement projects. Maintenance work is strongly supported by habit patterns and established procedures. There is a greater sense of urgency attached to both expected and unexpected maintenance work. Most of the items on our daily to-do lists are maintenance jobs. These are always on our minds, pressing for constant attention.

Most annual performance goals, however, refer to development

Figure 5-1. Maintenance-development analysis worksheet.

Maintenance-Development Work Analysis

Activity	D-M	Time	Dele? Elim?	Activity	D-M	Time	Dele? Elim?

issues. We know they are important, but they are not pressing for immediate attention. Here, again, we see the strain between the long range and the short range. Planning is the best strategy for balancing the two. Our planning must provide a way to make time available for all four combinations, whether on a daily, weekly, or monthly basis.

The Problem With To-Do Lists

Since the days of Charles Schwab, people have been using to-do lists. Since we began working with Time Management in the early 1970s, we have seen the number of to-do list users more than double. However, although most of us are using them, to-do lists are not as useful as we wish they were. They have not solved our time problems.

Part of the difficulty with to-do lists is the way we make the list. The following shows a typical example:

> Call BJ—contract
> Call Betty—expense policy
> Call Ed—computer problem
> Return call to Frank
> Return call to Sam
> Order newsletter
> Write Van—his new book finally published
> Write Katie—congrats on winning sales award
> Write Larry—meeting next month
> Write LTS—inquiry about our services
> Call Debbie—21st birthday
> Study month-end reports
> Plan conference presentation
> Staff meeting
> Mail convention registration
> Complete expense report

One reason many lists don't work is that they are poorly prepared, like the one above. The lists tend to consist of a random collection of activities, and some are several pages long. A few of the activities may relate to goals, but many are simply random events that have occurred on one day. The lists include everything from the key activities of the day to unimportant reminders such as "Buy a loaf of bread on the way home from the office." (Granted, the bread may be important at dinner-time.) Very few lists have any indication of priorities or estimates of how long it will take to accomplish the various tasks.

As a result, very few of us consistently accomplish all the items on our to-do list by the end of the day. Most of us complain that we carry more and more items over to the next day. We feel depressed and guilty as the list grows longer. It becomes a constant reminder of how far behind we are. In this case, of course, we can rightfully say that preparing a to-do list seems to make very little difference in the results they achieve.

A to-do list prepared in a haphazard manner is actually demotivating, guaranteeing future frustration. Seldom does the list maker accomplish all the items on the list. Thus each new list is simply a reminder of the disappointments to be faced by the end of the day. This strengthens people's conviction that writing things down has nothing to do with accomplishing them. It is frustrating to realize at the beginning of the day that all your intended work will probably not be finished. Further frustration results when, in fact, a number of the items are not finished by the end of the day. Continuing to write out a to-do list under these conditions is a futile gesture.

Two simple actions would improve the common to-do list. First, add priority codes to indicate what is most important. Second, add time estimates of how long each activity will require.

A	Call BJ—contract	15 min.
A	Call Betty—expense policy	20 "
	Call Ed—computer problem	20 "
A	Return call to Frank	5 "
A	Return call to Sam	5 "
	Order newsletter	15 "
	Write Van—his new book finally published	15 "
	Write Katie—congrats on winning sales award	10 "
	Write Larry—meeting next month	15 "
A	Write LTS—inquiry about our services	30 "
	Call Debbie—21st birthday	20 "
	Study month-end reports	30 "
A	Plan conference presentation	2 hrs.
	Staff meeting	1 "
	Mail convention registration	15 min.
A	Complete expense report	20 "

This list allows better planning. You can see what is most important, and how long it will take. If your list is too long, you will know right away, not just at the end of the day. You can consider alternatives, like delegating part of the work or delaying low-value items until later.

A Systematic Approach to Planning

The key to successful planning is to plan both work and time. At best, a to-do list is only a work plan. However, you usually run out of time, not work. A good plan must consider both.

Our systematic approach has six basic elements. To use this approach, simply ask yourself the following six questions:

1. *Results:* "What are my goals; what do I expect to accomplish?"
2. *Activities:* "What will I have to do to get those results?"
3. *Priorities:* "What are the priorities involved?"
4. *Time estimates:* "How much time will each activity require?"
5. *Schedules:* "When will I do each activity?"
6. *Flexibility:* "How much flexibility must I allow for the unexpected things I can't control?"

The answers to the first three questions form a work plan. The answers to the last three make a time plan. You need both types of plan (see Figure 5-2). The ordinary to-do list is neither. Most to-do lists address only question 2, but without focusing on specific goals. Only 30 percent of the to-do lists we have seen indicate any kind of priority code. Even then, most priority codes indicate only the urgency of the item, not its importance.

The Weekly Plan

A weekly plan is usually better than a daily plan for most of us, although few of us ever make one. It provides a longer perspective and allows more room for options. Lee Iacocca, in his autobiography, credits his weekly plan as his secret for being able to accomplish so much (*Iacocca: An Autobiography*, New York: Bantam Books, 1984). Ralph Cordiner, when he was president of General Electric, often said that if managers would only think several days in advance, they would avoid over half the problems that plague their days.

To prepare a weekly plan, ask the six basic planning questions for next week. If possible, do this at the end of the preceding week. For instance, you might take time out on Friday afternoon, or perhaps on the weekend. Preparing a weekly plan requires only about 30 minutes for most people, but it will enable them to recover at least an hour a

Figure 5-2.   The key components of a total time plan.

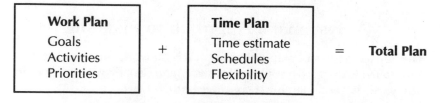

day next week. An extra hour or more every day for important work will produce remarkable results in almost any job.

Make sure your weekly goals are well defined before you proceed (see Chapter 2). As you write down your weekly goals, review your ongoing projects and look ahead to longer-range goals in order to keep your week in perspective.

Remember, you cannot *do* a goal. A goal is a result achieved over time. You can only do activities. If you do the right activities, you have a good chance of reaching your goals. If you do the wrong activities, you will probably not reach your goal. Determining what has to be done means thinking through all the activities necessary to accomplish each goal.

Setting priorities for all your activities is mandatory. Plans will not always work out in the way they are written. When changes become necessary, they should be built around the highest-priority items. If you fail to establish priorities, you may forget important actions in your rush to modify the plan. Base your priorities on the importance of the activity, not just on its urgency.

Most of us are hopelessly optimistic about how much can be done in any given time span. We are poor judges of time and generally underestimate how long a task will take. When we try to estimate the time for a total project, we tend to make our greatest errors.

A better approach is to break the project down into specific activities and estimate the completion time for each activity. When estimating completion times, you should always think in terms of absolute minimums. If you could work at a certain task without interruptions or distractions, how long would it take? This estimate should then form the basis for your time plan.

It is important to assign specific times to your tasks, especially the most important ones. Tasks or activities are never ending. There is always something else that can be done. Time is the limiting factor. There are never enough hours in a day for all the things that could be done. Therefore, a plan must be built around the most critical element—time.

As you consider the question of when things ought to be done, remember that there is a proper sequence for events. If things are done in the proper sequence, they take less time and produce better results. If they are done out of sequence, they inevitably create a great deal of wasted time before they are finally accomplished.

Where things are done can also have a major impact on whether or not they are achieved. For instance, a discussion taking place in your office is subject to any number of interruptions. If the discussion were to take place in a conference room, many of those interruptions could be avoided.

Figure 5-3 shows a worksheet for developing a weekly plan based on your prioritized goals. Note your goals at the top. Actions necessary to accomplish these goals are listed at the bottom. Next to each activity, note a priority value and an estimate of how much time the activity will take. Then, allocate the activities to the day on which they

Figure 5-3.   Weekly planner.

Weekly Planner

Week Beginning

GOALS: Results To Achieve This Week

Must Do This Week	PR	Time	Monday
			Tuesday
			Wednesday
			Thursday
Would Like To Do This Week	PR	Time	Friday
			Saturday/Sunday

should be done. Total all the time estimates to see if you have allowed enough flexibility in your week.

People often ask how much time they should allow for flexibility. The answer to this question depends on how much time you can control. Observation indicates that the range of controllable time can vary from 10 to 80 percent of total time.

A time log is the best way we know to determine how much flexibility you need. You must allow for all the unexpected things you can't control: interruptions, crises, telephone calls, requests from the boss, absent staff members, or changes in the weather. All these things will continue to happen. In spite of them, however, there still is a set of goals to accomplish.

Whenever the time required to accomplish goals is greater than the time available to accomplish them, something has to give. You may be tempted to say, "Well, they've all got to get done. I'll just have to squeeze everything together somehow." However, if the minimal times estimated for the activities are accurate, this is not a possibility. You simply can't do things in less time than they actually take. In addition, Murphy's second law reminds you that everything takes longer than you think it will . . . activities may not be accomplished within the estimated time.

Faced with this kind of difficulty, you have several options. You could revise the original plan, rescheduling some things for another week. You could delegate some tasks. You could look for ways to simplify the tasks, do them more efficiently. You could go into hiding for a while. You could work more hours than normal. If none of these options is feasible, then you will probably not reach your goals by the end of the week.

At this point an important difference should be noted between having a plan and not having a plan. Assume that you did not prepare a weekly plan. When would you be likely to discover that you have tackled more tasks than you can handle during the week? Probably Thursday or Friday. By then, however, it would be too late to do much about it. The purpose of thinking through the week and writing up a plan is to discover potential problems far enough in advance to do something about them.

Plan consistently, every week. Plan those weeks that seem to be too simple to require planning as well as those weeks when you think you are going to be too busy to plan. If you plan your time regularly every week, you will soon develop a habit of planning.

Is a weekly plan worth the effort? People who use them think so. They repeatedly tell us about ten benefits.

1. It forces them to think ahead.
2. It helps them avoid problems.

3. It helps streamline the work flow.
4. It provides them and others with more lead time.
5. It helps them better coordinate activities with others.
6. It helps them manage staff time better.
7. It helps them avoid overcommitment.
8. It helps them say no more often.
9. It helps them work more relaxed.
10. It helps them get more done.

The value of weekly planning cannot be overemphasized. The weekly plan is the backbone of any strategy to control time. People who consistently prepare a weekly plan get more accomplished than those who don't plan each week. Ironically, the fact that planners consistently produce better results than nonplanners has not been sufficient to cause people to plan more often.

Turning Slow Time Into Productive Time

Personnel executives were asked about the productivity rating for each hour of the week. Friday afternoon, between 4:00 P.M. and 5:00 P.M., was the worst hour of the week, with a productivity rating of only 2 percent! What a waste—and what an opportunity! If this is true at your organization, consider turning that hour into high-quality time.

At 4:00 P.M. sit down and prepare a plan for the next week. This will only take about a half hour for most people. Ask others around you to do the same.

At 4:30 P.M., meet together and share your plans for next week. Just spread them all out on a table, and have everyone look at everyone else's plan. As you are reviewing each other's plan for next week, look for connecting points with each other. Discuss how to coordinate your priorities and activities. If necessary, revise your plans.

This coordination meeting will only need about a half hour. So, at 5:00 P.M. you can all go home and relax for the weekend. You will already be in better shape for next week than most people ever are.

People trying this exercise tell us about the following eight benefits.

1. It helps keep the group focused.
2. It helps keep the group informed.
3. It helps balance priorities.
4. It increases the amount of information shared.
5. It helps avoid lots of problems.
6. It promotes good teamwork.

7. It helps boost performance levels.
8. It helps build morale.

This approach will work at any level of the organization. It works between superiors and subordinates. It works with peers. It works on project teams. It works with suppliers or customers. In fact, it works so well, you really ought to try it for yourself. You may find it so valuable you will feel like writing us a check for $25,000, just as Charles Schwab did. This small effort can be revolutionary!

The Daily Plan

Weekly planning does not negate the need for daily planning. You'll get best results when the two work together. Every day is simply one step in the week. Establish your goals for the day. Write out all the planned activities for accomplishing the day's goals. Rate them according to priority, and estimate the amount of time required for each one. Figure 5-4 shows a sample of a daily plan, including space to schedule activities, which we take up in the next chapter.

Now add to the list the other events that keep popping up. In all probability, many of these other activities will not relate directly to goals. You may have to do them anyway. However, preparing a daily plan in this fashion gives you the opportunity to compare important activities with unimportant activities. With things spelled out in black and white on a list, you may find it easier to let the unimportant things go until you have attended to the important things first.

When should you do your daily planning? Preferably at the end of the preceding day. Your daily plan should be completed before you arrive at the office in the morning. There are several good reasons for this.

First, reviewing the day you have just completed helps you when preparing the list for the next day. What went right today? What went wrong? Were things in control or out of control? How can you do better tomorrow? This quick review at the end of the day helps you prepare a better list for tomorrow. The details of the day will be fresher in your mind at the end of the day than they will be tomorrow morning. It also lets you clear your mind so you can enjoy your evening more.

Second, planning in advance gives you a psychological head start. While you are preparing for your day and commuting to the office, you can go over all the points on your plan for today. You will be ready to swing into action the moment you arrive at the office.

Third, a plan prepared in advance gives you a comparison base

Figure 5-4.   Daily planner.

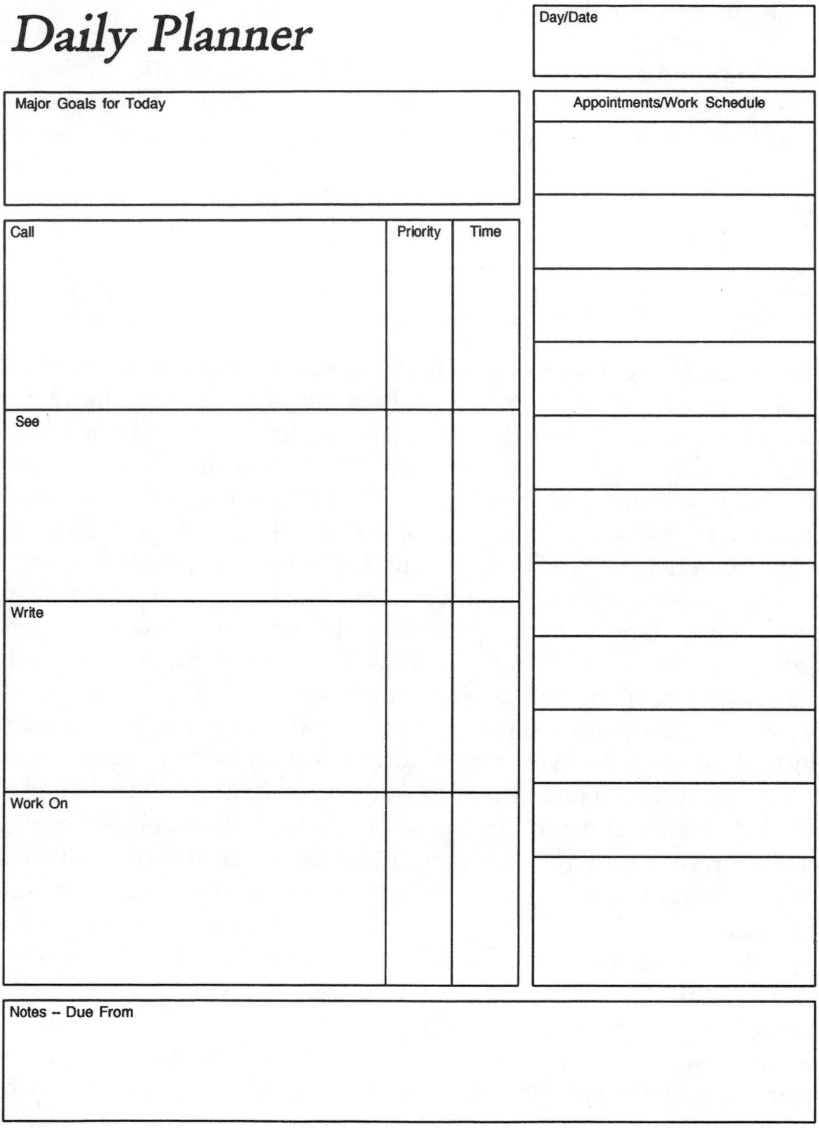

Daily Planner

Day/Date

Major Goals for Today			Appointments/Work Schedule

Call	Priority	Time

See		

Write		

Work On		

Notes – Due From

right from the beginning. Without such a plan, you are likely to be trapped by half a dozen things that are already coming unglued the moment you walk through the door. You will probably get engaged in them immediately. With a plan, however, you might pause to say, "Is this item more important or less important than what I have planned?" If it is more important, by all means do it. If it is less important, think for a moment about how you might ignore it, say no, reschedule it for later, or otherwise avoid it. A daily plan is a useful curb on extraneous activities. It keeps you on track for your goals. Of course, you can still "jump the curb," but you have an extra measure of protection if you conscientiously prepare the plan daily.

Planning is a central factor in all time-management success stories. It is a road map to accomplishment and an exercise in freedom. Planning leads to results, for it gives you control over your most valuable resource—time.

Choosing the Right Notebook Organizer/ Planner System

People repeatedly ask two questions: "Should I use one of the notebook organizer/planner systems?" and if so, "Which one do you recommend?" The answer to the first question is easy—yes, we recommend using them. The answer to the second, though, is more difficult.

There are dozens of planning and organizing notebook systems on the market. More are arriving every month. Most are useful, although some are better than others. The best answer of which one to buy is this: Choose the one you will actually use.

The difficulty in recommending one is that we don't know enough about you. Do you want one for your work, your personal life, or both? What size do you prefer? Will you be carrying it around or leaving it on your desk? How many projects are you involved in? How many details must you track? What is your predominant work style?

However, here are some things to consider:

• *The eight common elements of a good organizer/planner.* For twenty years, we've been studying how people work, how they use their time, and how they can work smarter. We've seen just about every planner and organizer there is. The good ones have about eight common elements:

1. A yearly calendar
2. A monthly calendar big enough to make notes on each day
3. Planning sheets for each day
4. A telephone and address section

5. A set of A–Z tabs
6. A set of other tabs with labels you can customize
7. A variety of specialized forms or worksheets
8. A sheet for keeping track of notes and discussions with others

Any notebook product that omits one or more of these basic elements would be less flexible and probably less useful.

• *Format.* With systems that have all these elements, the next set of criteria concerns the format of the daily planning sheets. These sheets should direct you to:

1. Identify specific activities.
2. Set priorities for activities.
3. Estimate the time needed for each activity.
4. Schedule the activities.

• *Time estimates.* Most notebook systems omit the time estimates. However, without them, you won't know whether your plan is realistic. Remember, you run out of time, not activities.

• *Ability to customize.* Finally, any notebook planner/organizer should allow you to customize. The most successful users have all customized their notebooks in many ways. Three-ring notebooks allow the greatest flexibility for customizing.

Use these guidelines to help sort out the different products and you will probably pick the one that is right for you. However, remember that the notebook is not the system. The notebook is only a set of forms, a tool. The system is independent of the forms. Time management depends less on the tools used and more on how you use the tools. Our system for managing time is based on the six questions discussed earlier in this chapter. It is compatible with any notebook product currently on the market.

The cost, color, size, shape, and weight, of course, are unimportant. You can be a great planner on cheap note paper and a dismal planner with a computerized notebook system costing hundreds of dollars. The secret is you—and your commitment to planning. Remember: Those who plan, accomplish more. Those who fail to plan may be accidental successes in the short term but will eventually fall into chaos as conditions and competition close in on them. Plan your own course. Plan for success. In the words of the old cliché, "If you're failing to plan, you're planning to fail."

Scoring Guide for Chapter Five Quiz					
	SA	**MA**	**U**	**MD**	**SD**
1.	5	4	3	2	1
2.	5	4	3	2	1
3.	5	4	3	2	1
4.	1	2	3	4	5

Six
Scheduling Activities

Nothing ever happens in your life unless you create the space for it to happen in.

James McCay,
The Management of Time

Before reading this chapter, please circle your response to each of the following statements. A scoring guide is at the end of the chapter.

SA = Strongly Agree   **MA** = Mildly Agree   **U** = Undecided
MD = Mildly Disagree   **SD** = Strongly Disagree

		Score
1. I schedule a specific time each day for doing the most important tasks.	SA MA U MD SD	_____
2. I often get distracted from my schedule and tend to jump from one task to another.	SA MA U MD SD	_____
3. I have a quiet time every day so I can concentrate on important work.	SA MA U MD SD	_____
4. I maintain flexibility by allowing time in my daily schedule for unexpected things.	SA MA U MD SD	_____
	Total Score	_____

Many people use the terms *planning* and *scheduling* interchangeably. Actually, the two words refer to two different activities. Planning is deciding what to do. Scheduling is deciding when to do it. Each day, as you schedule the events that will fill your hours, you must carefully chart that dangerous path between Parkinson and Murphy.

Parkinson's law reminds you that work expands to fill the time available for its accomplishment. This means that if you allow too much time for a task, the task will take up all the time that you allow. Murphy's second law, though, cautions you that everything seems to take longer than you think it will. This means that if you do not allow adequate time for a task, the task will take as much time as it needs anyway. In either case, your schedule will be upset. Your challenge is to allow enough time, but not too much time, for every task you undertake.

Constructing a Schedule

A schedule is more than a to-do list, although many people assume it is the same thing. A to-do list is an itemization of activities that must be done today. Following our advice from Chapter Five, you would add appropriate priorities and a time estimate for each activity. However, if the activities are to be done, the question is when—at what precise time. That's where scheduling comes in. Scheduling is simply to pick a time to do the activities.

Your schedule should start with the most important activities from your to-do list, or daily plan. Look at any appointments, standing meetings, or committees, and similar items that you know will have to take place at a particular time. Block these out of your schedule. These items are fixed unless you realistically have the option of not doing them, or have sufficient reasons to change them.

People anticipate the most problems with two scheduling steps: estimating time needs and scheduling specific times for activities. Estimating time is a skill. Most of us do it so little that we have not developed the skill. However, you can become an expert at estimating time needs within a month or so. The more you do it, the better you get. When you begin estimating time needs, you automatically pay more attention to how long jobs really take, what's actually involved.

Scheduling, we say, is just not possible. Things just don't work out the way we intend them to. You can't anticipate what's going to happen on any given day. Truth is, we notice that at least half the things we schedule work out exactly as planned, right from the very beginning. This is another skill. The more you work at it, the better you get. The more you try to schedule, the more you learn about how to schedule in your particular situation.

Scheduling is the secret of making things happen. Planning is only an intention; scheduling is more like a commitment. Things that are scheduled tend to happen—and happen on time. Things that are not scheduled may never happen. If you want them to happen, schedule them.

The two most scheduled items in American business are meetings and lunch. Both of these activities take place regularly, whether worthwhile or not. It's common sense. If you want people to get together at the same time, you have to schedule it. What we don't schedule is work we do alone. Yet, that is the work that we struggle most to find time for. Stop struggling, and start scheduling.

Think for a moment: What do you wish you had more time for? Common responses include planning, improving procedures, research and analysis, thinking, and learning. Wait a minute: "Schedule time for thinking and learning?" Yes! If you want to get time for it. Yet, few of us actually schedule time for these activities. That is one big reason why they don't occur as often as we wish they did. Experiment a bit. Try scheduling the activities you wish you had more time for, and see if you don't spend more time doing them.

Put Your Schedule in Writing

Here's a requirement that many of us tend to skip over: A schedule should be written. You simply can't remember everything you're planning to do—or when you plan to do it—in the midst of a hectic day. The schedule should be on a single sheet, not on numerous little notes. If you keep little notes, you will be shuffling paper all day long—and losing some along the way as they fall off your desk, out of your pocket, or who knows what else. Refer to Figure 5-4 for a sample of a daily planning and scheduling form.

Writing things down helps you clarify your thoughts and focus on what you're trying to accomplish with the day. It will increase your commitment to your daily goals and let you spot problems or faults in logic before they lead you astray. A written schedule is also a handy point of reference after you have handled interruptions and unexpected events. You won't have to think about what you should do next; you already have it on your schedule. Simply go to it and do it. Be certain to keep the schedule visible at all times. Don't tuck it in a drawer, your pocket, or your briefcase. Keep it on the desk, or stick it on the wall in front of you. Put it in a spot where you'll be sure to see it frequently.

Your list should be a constant reminder of what you ought to be doing and how your day should be progressing. Don't think of it as a tyrant telling you what to do. Rather, realize that it is your only key to keeping your sanity and getting things accomplished.

Maintain Flexibility

The biggest scheduling mistake you can make is to allocate every minute of your day. This approach is guaranteed to fail. You can seldom control the entire day. Although it is possible occasionally, you cannot count on it happening very often. There are just too many unexpected things that make demands on your time. You must leave room for the unexpected when you are constructing your schedule. Most people know that they will be interrupted during the day, but very few actually plan for interruptions. Remember, interruptions are a part of your job. Planning for interruptions means leaving room in your schedule for them.

How much flexibility should you allow? There is no definite answer to this question. You may only need 10 to 20 percent of the day for unexpected items. On the other hand, we've seen some people who need as much as 50 to 70 percent of the day for unexpected activities. You will have to determine the appropriate amount of flexible time for yourself. Keeping a time log of your job for a week or two can help you determine how much flexibility your job demands.

The amount of flexibility required in your job depends on several factors. The more people there are around you and the more you interact with others, the more flexibility you will need. Self-discipline is another factor. If you are highly disciplined in your work habits, you probably won't need as much flexibility as a less disciplined individual. The amount of "noise" around you also affects flexibility. The more you work in isolation, the less flexibility you will need, since you will probably have fewer interruptions and distractions.

There are several ways to build flexibility into your schedule. Figure 6-1 illustrates several common scheduling patterns. Many people prefer Pattern A, which offers a distinct advantage over the others. With Pattern A, if things do work out according to schedule, you have a large block of unscheduled time available in the afternoon. With the other patterns, even when things work out well, your gained time is scattered throughout the day. An entire afternoon would allow you to tackle another special project, analyze parts of your operation, catch up on your reading, or do any number of things that you simply couldn't do as well in little blocks of time. An available afternoon may give you an opportunity to work on your long-range plans or explore a new opportunity. Occasionally it may even allow you a round of golf. An increasing number of people are gaining additional personal time by finding ways to accomplish their goals earlier in the day than usual.

Remember Parkinson's law as you're trying to decide which flex-

Figure 6-1.   Scheduling patterns.

Pattern		Morning	Afternoon

Key: ▨ Scheduled   ☐ Unscheduled

ibility pattern to use. Work does expand. Even if you do find yourself with a slack period, you may waste the time trying to decide what to do next. Therefore, you should always have at least one alternative plan prepared for those days when the unexpected—surprisingly—doesn't happen.

One thing you might do on those occasional days is to gain on tomorrow's list. You may also want to develop an "opportunity" list ahead of time. On most days you will need all the time you have just to take care of the unexpected, but on those days when the unexpected doesn't happen, you should have plans for adequately using that gained time. If there isn't anything significant for you to do, maybe you should take a long lunch hour instead. If you hang around the office when you don't have anything to do, you may "goof off" and prevent other people from accomplishing their goals for the day.

When you consider possible scheduling options, remember to keep your goals in mind. You may be required, for example, to attend a particular staff meeting. You know from past experience that the meeting is usually unproductive. Attending the meeting will hinder your efforts to achieve good results from your day. On the other hand, you want to survive in the organization. What do you do? You can try to make the meeting worthwhile. If that is not possible, you may be able to skip a meeting from time to time without serious consequences. It is usually unwise, though, to miss all the meetings. Therefore, you will have to consider some unproductive meeting time as part of your job. You may as well block it out on your schedule and work around it. Concentrate on using the balance of your time effectively.

Whatever you do, match your schedule to the realities of your job. And here's a very important suggestion that works for almost everyone: Try to schedule the morning as tightly as possible. Make sure the first hour of your day is a productive one; you can read the newspaper later. The first hour sets a pattern for the day. If you get a good start, things will go better all day. If you get a poor start, you'll spend all day trying to catch up.

Group Related Items

Don't make your day any more fragmented or hectic than it already is. If you have a number of phone calls to make, try to handle them all at the same time. If you have to write a number of letters, try to dictate all of them at the same time. If you group related items in your schedule, you will not have to make as many psychological shifts during the day, and the day will seem easier. Even if your phone calls relate to different things, handling all the calls at one time will put you in a telephone frame of mind. If you intersperse telephone-letters-telephone-meeting-letters-telephone, you will have much more difficulty focusing your activities and your efforts.

Use Minijobs for Minigaps

To get more done during the day, take advantage of small time gaps. For instance, you have just finished a report. It is 11:39, and you must leave for a lunch appointment at 11:45. Six minutes are too short to tackle anything new, so you just putter around doing nothing for six minutes.

There are dozens of these mini time gaps in a day. They may happen when you have to wait, between major tasks, or after interruptions before you get back to what you were doing before. Learning to use these small time gaps can put you way ahead. Herbert Hoover wrote an entire book in hundreds of fifteen-minute intervals.

The key is to prepare ahead of time how to use these gaps when they occur. Simply list all the tasks you can do in five to ten minutes. Some people even make a second list of jobs that can be done in fifteen to thirty minutes.

It's amazing how many jobs can be done in only five to ten minutes. You could make a phone call, look up phone numbers for later calls, or write a memo. You could file papers, read a report or make a to-do list. You might make notes on a project, schedule appointments, or make flight reservations. You can make a list of what you can do in five to ten minutes. Even if you can't finish an entire project, you can often move it steadily ahead a few minutes at a time.

Whenever you find yourself facing another mini time gap, just fill it with a minijob. You will find it helps you get more accomplished during the day.

Make Transition Time Productive

Transition time is the space between events and consists mostly of waiting time or travel time. Your time log will show how much time you normally spend in each category. Travel time is discussed in Chapter Nine.

Many people think of waiting time as a gift, an uninterrupted spot of time they had not planned on. They use it for catching up on their reading, doing some planning, or reviewing things that they never seem to find the time for. You should always have alternative activities in mind so that when you are faced with waiting time you won't waste it trying to figure out what to do. Not only will you be rewarded by getting something done, but you'll feel less frustrated by having to wait.

Don't forget to make all your trips around the office count. As you walk from office to office, try to use the time productively. Return reports to the file, water a plant, or even conduct a walking meeting with another person.

Stick to the Schedule

A plan and schedule for the day is no good unless you follow it. Do you spend your day pursuing your goals, or do you spend your day chasing rabbits, jumping up and pursuing anything that catches your attention? It is one thing to know what you are after; it is quite another to achieve it. Learn to control your unscheduled action impulses. Don't chase rabbits.

Do anything you can to avoid activity traps. Don't engage in random activities. Before you add anything to your schedule, think about its purpose. Most people are far too casual in their work habits. Use your schedule as a way to help you develop better habits.

When something unexpected arises, do not automatically take off after it. Stop and ask yourself, "Is this unexpected event more important than what I had planned to do instead?" If it is more important, go right ahead and pursue it. You should always focus on the most important items before you tackle the less important ones. But if the unexpected event is not more important, try to reschedule it for another time, ignore it, say no, or do anything else that will enable you to engage in more important activities. Whenever possible, stay on your planned course. The rewards will be great.

Say No When You Should

One of the biggest causes for busted schedules and time pressure is our inability to say no. Saying no can be difficult, almost impossible for some. For instance, it is hard for unassertive people to say no, even when they realize it is the best response. It is hard for most of us to say no when our boss is asking. However, failure to say no creates problems.

Many people work sixty, seventy, even eighty hours a week. Few of them enjoy working that many hours. Many of them feel that the company takes advantage of them. Yet, they seldom stop to consider that they have helped trap themselves.

Suppose your boss comes by one afternoon and asks you to tackle another special project. You respond, "Yes. I'll get on it right away." The boss goes away happy, believing that all is well.

What you should have said is, "I'd really love to do that, but do you realize everything I'm already involved in? Which tasks do you want me to set aside in order to tackle this new assignment?" If you really are loaded up and you fail to say so, you are contributing to your own downfall.

We complain that our boss ought to know how busy we are without our having to say anything. That would be nice, but it is unrealistic. Truth is, many bosses won't ever know unless you say so . . . or unless you fail to deliver results on time. Learning about a problem early is always better than learning about it later.

So, speak up. People don't do their best work when they are feeling the time pressures of overcommitment.

Let Others Help With Your Schedule

Meet with your secretary or assistant for a few minutes every morning to review goals, priorities, and planned actions for the day. A brief afternoon meeting may also help keep things in focus or make necessary adjustments in your schedule. The more your staff knows what you are trying to achieve today, the more they can help.

You might even consider having your secretary or assistant schedule your time for you. There are two good reasons for this. First of all, another person can say no much more easily than you can. If you have staff available who can schedule your time, why not let them try doing so?

Schedule Quiet Time

If you work in an office, your days are probably hectic, fragmented, and frustrating. An endless stream of interruptions makes it difficult to get things done. The constant start-and-stop-and-restart pattern stretches jobs out longer than necessary. It often reduces the quality of your work. You accomplish only about half of what you should be able to do with a working day. Quiet time can change all this.

Most people these days favor quiet time. In fact they find quiet time so helpful that they come to work early or stay late to be sure they have at least one private hour to themselves. They assume quiet time isn't possible during the day, so they don't even try. Figure 6-2 shows a comparison of executive time patterns in four countries. Which pattern do you suppose would be the best for getting more accomplished during the day?

In his study, Professor Doktor found that Japanese executives spent almost half their day working in segments of more than sixty minutes. American executives, on the other hand, spent only about 10 percent of the day in segments of that length. Most people would rather have the Japanese pattern. The question is how to do it.

Quiet time is simple: Create an uninterrupted block of time so you can concentrate on your work. This usually means turning off the telephone and blocking drop-in visitors for a while. Close your door, turn off your telephone, find an empty conference room, go to the library, or do whatever you must. One man who works in an open office space simply dons a red baseball cap to signal that his "door" is shut. It works.

What do people actually do during quiet time? They think. They plan. They get organized. They do analytical work, write reports, or work on projects that require creativity. One big plus is that in one hour of quiet time, they can get as much done as they could in three or four hours of regular time.

Be careful not to abuse the quiet-time concept. You can't isolate yourself all day. However, most of us can afford to be unavailable for

Figure 6-2. International comparison of executive work segments.

Percentage of time spent working in blocks of . . .	Japan	Korea	Hong Kong	USA
Less than 9 minutes	14%	10%	37%	49%
9–60 minutes	42	48	51	41
Over 60 minutes	44	42	12	10

Source: Robert Doktor, "Asian and American CEOs: A Comparative Study," *Organizational Dynamics* (Winter 1990): 45–56.

an hour or so once or twice a day. Test it and see for yourself how to make it work best for you. Quiet time is an excellent way to increase your productivity without increasing your hours. Write to us, and we'll send you an attractive sign to help you create some quiet time for yourself.

Create Group Quiet Time

Individuals can, and do, implement quiet time on their own, but the greatest benefits occur when groups do it together. An entire office, department, division, or company can help make all employees successful when they observe quiet time as a unit.

Everyone should be included. Everyone in the office makes a special effort to do their work quietly and not bother coworkers. No one calls anyone else. No one drops in on anyone else. There are not meetings scheduled. External interruptions are minimized whenever possible.

Michigan Miller's Mutual Insurance Company has enjoyed the benefits of a companywide quiet hour for many years. In 1962, Charles McGill, president of the company, noticed that many of his employees began the workday with nonproductive chatter. "They rehashed the soap operas and the ball games," he remembers. "Other workers would complain that it was difficult for them to concentrate." So, long before quiet hours became a well-known idea, Mr. McGill instituted a quiet hour policy from 8:00 to 9:00 A.M. and from 1:00 to 2:00 P.M. in one division of his company. The experiment worked so well that in 1966, the quiet hour became a policy throughout the organization. The afternoon quiet hour was dropped, but the morning policy is still in effect. At 8:00 A.M. sharp a single announcement is heard over the public-address system: "Good morning." All conversation and idle chatter quickly stop—people go to work. "We all do it," one employee reported, "from the president to the custodians. That's what makes it work so well; we all do it together!"

Company employees appear to be as enthusiastic about the quiet hour as the company president. "We were told about the policy during our first employment interview," one secretary explained. "At first I thought it was a little childish, like being in elementary school; but now I know it works and I like it a lot." Frequent callers to the office are aware of the quiet hour each morning and voluntarily refrain from calling unless absolutely necessary. Of course, emergencies are handled when they need to be. As one employee pointed out, "This isn't a rigid system. It just helps us all get something accomplished with our day."

Experiment on your own. Pick a time when things are normally slower. Most offices experience a relatively slow period somewhere during the day. It often occurs between 8:00 and 9:00 A.M., 11:30 A.M. and 1:30 P.M., and 4:00 and 5:00 P.M. Investigate the activity patterns in your own office.

To successfully implement a quiet time in your organization, follow these nine steps:

1. Secure firm commitment from the top managers of the unit.
2. Discuss the concept with everyone, focusing on the benefits, and secure their commitment.
3. Determine what time period is most appropriate.
4. Develop operating guidelines.
5. Try quiet time first as a pilot project.
6. Monitor results, and solve problems as they arise.
7. Evaluate results of the pilot project.
8. Modify operating guidelines.
9. Implement quiet time as a regular policy.

The key to group quiet time is to keep exceptions to a bare minimum. The biggest questions concern what to do about customer calls. Most companies accept calls from customers whenever they occur. They never tell customers not to call. However, in almost every case, when customers discover what the company is doing, many of them voluntarily stop calling during those times. If quiet time can successfully block all the internal interruptions, the problem has been significantly reduced.

Consider Body Time

Most of us think of ourselves as either morning people or night people. It is true that our bodies are in better position to tackle certain kinds of tasks at particular times of day. For instance, morning people seem able to do creative work best early in the day, while night people prefer to do creative work in the evening. If it is possible for you to schedule your day to take advantage of your natural moods, by all means do so.

Be sure, though, that you really are a morning or night person and have not simply talked yourself into it. It is possible that your behavior has become a self-fulfilling prophecy. If you state a belief and then act according to it, you justify the belief. You act to fulfill your own expectations. Rearranging your expectations may allow you to discover new truths about yourself.

If you do not function well in the morning, ask yourself if you are starting your day properly. Many people begin their workday with inadequate sleep and poor nutrition. They wake up tired. Breakfast consists of a cup of coffee and perhaps a piece of toast. Then they attempt to start the day successfully.

Under these conditions, the body's blood sugar level is at its lowest point. Breakfast should bring your body up to full functioning capacity. If you sleep more and eat better, you may discover that you can be extremely productive and creative in early morning.

Dr. Dorothy Tennov, a personal management consultant in Millsboro, Delaware, suggests that people have different mental energy levels at different times of the day (*Super Self*, New York: Funk & Wagnalls, 1976). Her research identifies five capability levels:

1. *Peak Level.* You're in top form. You are more creative, get more ideas, and can learn new things better.
2. *Good level.* You're better than average, but not at your best. You can do most things at this level.
3. *Average level.* You can carry out complex activities, providing you aren't trying to learn them. Most people are here for most of the day.
4. *Relaxed, pleasant level.* You can function well if you stick to easy things.
5. *Low level.* Good for low-level activity as long as you don't have to think or make decisions.

If you want to perform more effectively, learn to be more aware of your basic energy patterns. Begin by listing your activities in a notebook. You could combine this with doing a time log. Alongside each activity, note the mental energy level that you feel you need to perform the task well. Also indicate the minimum level you would find acceptable to handle each activity.

As your energy levels rise and fall, try to do each activity at the lowest level possible, saving your higher levels for more demanding tasks. You are definitely wasting energy, and probably time, if you do mundane tasks during peak levels.

It isn't necessary to completely reschedule your day to put your energy levels to better use. Being aware of your patterns can keep you from misusing your energy. Just remember that while low-level tasks can be accomplished at high energy levels, the reverse is seldom true. If you try an activity requiring peak-level energy when you're at your lowest point, you are unlikely to get good results.

Get an Early Start

Everyone knows that starting early is good advice, but we don't all follow it. Even our old proverbs talk about the value of starting early.

As the first hour of the day goes, so goes the day.

The early bird gets the worm.

The early hours have gold in their mouth.

Early to bed and early to rise, makes a man healthy, wealthy, and wise.

How we start definitely helps determine how we finish. Get a good, productive start and you're more likely to have a successful, productive day. Get a poor start and you'll be playing catch-up all day. No matter what happens you'll feel behind all day long. As you hurry and struggle to catch up, another old saying applies: "The hurrier I go, the behinder I get."

Starting early can give you a psychological edge, a head start, and perhaps more luck. People who start early tend to be in the right place at the right time more often. Some say they are luckier than the rest of us. Maybe it has more to do with good judgment or good habits.

Starting early can have three different meanings. First, it might mean starting the day at an earlier hour. Many people find this beneficial. Second, it might mean starting to work when you get to work. Don't waste the first hour of the day on coffee, conversation, or newspapers. Third, it might mean starting on projects earlier than you normally would, giving yourself more lead time.

An early start will be easier if you train yourself to concentrate your thoughts in the early morning. Put your subconscious to work for you. While you're preparing to leave the house, or while you commute to work, focus your thoughts on your daily plan. Review your most important tasks. Think about the things that are most likely to upset your day. Consider what you would do if those things did happen. Visualize yourself at the end of a successful day. Psychologically, you will already have begun your day by the time you get to work. You're also more likely to go immediately to the important tasks for the day.

Good organization also helps you start early. Lay out things you'll need the night before. Pull files or other materials before you leave the office tonight. Lay out your clothes for tomorrow before you go to bed. Make the kid's school lunches tonight. Do anything you can to make the morning go smoothly. Quite often, minor preparations will make a big difference. Even a few minutes the night before can prevent major hassles the next morning.

Examine Your Opening Exercises

Our habit patterns play an important role in scheduling activities. Because we are so accustomed to doing the same thing all the time, we do it without thinking. Habits may be unconsciously scheduled activities. An important example of this kind of patterned behavior is the early-morning ritual in many offices—what we call opening exercises. What activities take place during the first thirty to sixty minutes, and how valuable are they? Consider Fred's typical morning. He drives down Center Street and turns right at the light. He parks in the third row of the parking lot, fourth space in—almost as though his name were engraved on the location. He enters his office at 8:00 A.M. The first thing he does is to get a cup of coffee; then he visits with his colleagues. As he finishes the coffee, he picks up the morning newspaper and browses through it for ten or fifteen minutes. It is now 8:45 A.M. Fred has been in the office for nearly an hour, but he hasn't started to work yet.

This pattern is probably repeated in over half the offices in the country every morning. "But wait a minute!" you may say. "There's nothing wrong with coffee, is there? Besides, talking with colleagues develops good interpersonal relationships." This may be true, but let's examine the above scenario in more detail.

We do not drink coffee for its nutritive value. Coffee is a social event, drinking is habitual behavior, often cued by morning entrance to the office. Coffee is also a social drink and generally cues us, especially in the early morning, to "shoot the breeze" with one another. What do we talk about? Early morning conversations usually center on sports, weather, family activities, television, and current events. These coffee conversations seldom concern work.

If coffee doesn't signal conversation, it signals the newspaper. In Fred's case, it signaled both. We read the sports page, comics, classified ads, and perhaps the front page. Very few businesses truly profit from employees' daily review of the morning paper, although we justify this habit as "keeping up with what's happening in the world."

Coffee, conversation, and newspapers aren't the only culprits during the opening-exercise period. Many of us do nothing more important than rearranging the things on our desks, opening the mail, sharpening our pencils, watering the plants, arranging lunch get-togethers with friends or any of the other trivial tasks we call "getting ready to get started."

As the old proverb says, "As the first hour of the day goes, so goes the day." This concept is vitally important to everyone concerned with good time management. Many of us waste our first hour, accomplishing little or nothing and establishing a poor pattern for the balance of the day. Furthermore, we don't even realize what we're doing to ourselves.

Prepare Your Schedule Before Arriving at Work

You should prepare your schedule before you arrive at the office in the morning. If you don't prepare your schedule beforehand, you have already blown your chance for a terrific start. Also, you run the risk of beginning your day by reacting to things already taking place when you arrive. You will lose your psychological advantage. With a schedule already prepared, you have the opportunity to stop and think for a moment before reacting.

There is another advantage to having your schedule prepared the evening before. As you go through your morning exercises of dressing, eating, and commuting to work, you can begin rehearsing the day around your schedule. With these preliminaries, you are far more likely to have the day work out as scheduled. For example, many salespeople have discovered that they consistently sell more when they know to whom their first call will be before leaving home in the morning.

Schedule Around Key Events

If you have one major goal, work that goal into your schedule first, then schedule everything else around the activities necessary to accomplish that goal. If, for instance, you know that an evaluation team from the home office is going to be in and out of your office over the next two or three days, build those activities into your schedule first. Then work all the other things that you hope to accomplish during the same period into your schedule. If you do not do this, the key event will be far more disruptive than it need be.

Developing Your Scheduling Skills

Scheduling is a skill, and like any skill, it can be learned. The more often you practice it, the more likely you are to become good at it. The better you are at scheduling your time, the more likely it is that your day will work out according to schedule.

To develop your scheduling skills, compare what you have scheduled for a given day with what actually happened. How did you do? What went right? What went wrong? Why? Could you have reasonably anticipated some of the unexpected events that threw your day off? Should you have used contingency plans during different parts of the day? If things were out of control, was it your fault or someone else's? For example, were you late getting into the office or did you take too long for lunch? Begin examining the differences between how you think the day ought to go and how the day actually goes and you will develop more skill at determining how to make things happen right. You will automatically accomplish more each day.

The key to scheduling is the belief that there is a time and a place for everything. Scheduling allows you to consider the appropriate time and place ahead of time, while you still have an opportunity to do something about it. Scheduling allows you to operate purposefully rather than randomly. You are likely to get more accomplished in less time and to have more time left over for yourself to do other things that are also important.

But remember, you cannot control everything. Many things are simply beyond your control. If you can consistently control 25 to 50 percent of your day, you will do well. If you fail to control whatever time you can, you will diminish your effectiveness. Whether you can take charge of eight hours a day or one hour a day is, in a sense, irrelevant. The idea is to control whatever time you can control. Remember, too, that you can manage much more of your day than you realize. Scheduling helps you to determine exactly how much of your day is controllable and helps you discover ways to approach time with authority—to achieve the results you desire.

The Psychology of Being Productive

Everyone knows the economic benefits from greater productivity. Scheduling activities is one of the keys to getting more done with your time—and to increasing productivity. Although the economic gains are certainly significant, the psychological aspects of improved productivity are equally potent. Consider what increased productivity can mean to you personally. Think back to one of those days when nothing seemed to go right. You ran in circles all day, and by 5:00 P.M. you had accomplished exactly nothing. How did you feel? Tired? Frustrated? Cranky? You may have gone home, kicked the cat, yelled at your kids, crabbed at your spouse, and collapsed.

In contrast, think of a day when everything went right. You piled success upon success. By 5:00 P.M. you had accomplished a great deal. How did you feel? Great? Exhilarated? Satisfied? Confident? You probably went home that day, played with the cat, hugged the kids, and took your spouse out for dinner, and maybe even a little dancing.

Did you work any longer or harder on that day than on any other? Probably not. What accounted for the difference in the way you felt, in your outlook on life? The answer, of course, is your sense of accomplishment.

We all want to feel that we are doing something important, making a contribution. Planning and scheduling our activities is one of the best ways to make sure we achieve more. The psychological payoff is tremendous. Achievers live better, and productivity is good for the psyche.

Scoring Guide for Chapter Six Quiz				
SA	**MA**	**U**	**MD**	**SD**
1. 5	4	3	2	1
2. 1	2	3	4	5
3. 5	4	3	2	1
4. 5	4	3	2	1

Seven
Streamlining Paperwork

A continuing flow of paper is sufficient to continue the flow of paper.

Dyer's law,
The Official Rules

Before reading this chapter, please circle your response to each of the following statements. A scoring guide is at the end of the chapter.

SA = Strongly Agree **MA** = Mildly Agree **U** = Undecided
MD = Mildly Disagree **SD** = Strongly Disagree

Score

1. I have a good systematic
   procedure for sorting and
   handling my paperwork. SA MA U MD SD _____

2. I often analyze my paperwork SA MA U MD SD _____
   and look for ways to
   eliminate, simplify, or improve
   it.

3. I use a tickler file or some SA MA U MD SD _____
   similar system to help keep
   track of details and maintain
   proper follow-up.

4. My desk or work area is rather SA MA U MD SD _____
   cluttered and should be
   neater.

Total Score _____

Can you imagine your job without paper? If it were only true! Paper is the essence of work for many of us. Even the computer age, which some dreamers claimed would eliminate the need for paper, has only increased our paper chores. Yet, how much of your paperwork would you say is truly worthwhile?

Unfortunately, if you guess that the majority of your paperwork is worthwhile, you're probably wrong. Studies have shown that most of the paper we handle at work is worthless. Only about 20 to 40 percent is truly worthwhile. You need to find that rich vein of gold within your paper mountain.

The bad news is that paperwork is increasing in most jobs. According to one study, the rate of increase is at least 20 percent annually. That means that your paperwork could double over a five-year period. No wonder you're having so much trouble struggling to stay on top of it.

Paper is also the essence of clutter. Many people pile, reshuffle, and pile again. They readily admit they need to get their paper better organized. However, this will often produce only small gains. There is simply too much paper. Reducing paper, not reorganizing it, is the key.

It's time to declare war on paper! To master your paper mountain you must relentlessly attack it on every front. There can be no retreat, no holding action. You must attack, move forward, and show no mercy. Now, read carefully; here's your battle plan.

Cleaning Up Your Desk

Begin the paperwork war at your desk. Chances are it could stand cleaning up. Don't get defensive, and don't excuse a messy desk by claiming, "That's just the way I am." You don't have to be perfect, but you can learn to be different, to be better.

Don Aslett, efficiency expert and author of *Not for Packrats Only* (New York: Plume Books, 1991) says, "Ninety percent of the time, messy desk people are less efficient, less in control, and less respected." Sure, your personality might shudder a bit at the thought of a neat desk, but, trust us—and give a neat desk a try.

To begin cleaning up your desk, schedule a block of time when you can work without interruption. You may need several hours. For most people, this means tackling their desk after regular office hours in the evening or on the weekend. If you must, make a midnight party out of it. Order a pizza and turn on the radio.

Be sure to have several large wastebaskets or plastic trash bags.

Maybe the janitor can provide those huge trash barrels with wheels on the bottom. However you do it, you will need space for lots of trash. Cleaning up your desk means getting rid of everything you can.

Scoop everything together in an exposed, central location. Collect all the stuff from the top of your desk, credenza, bookcases, filing cabinets, and tables. Don't forget stuff piled on the floor or sitting on window ledges. For a complete job, take everything out of your desk drawers, too.

Emptying your desk may reveal dozens of nonpaper items: staples, pencils, rulers, nondairy creamer, soup, aspirins, scissors, erasers, adhesive tape, old sweaters, cassettes, plaques, paperweights, paper clips, stamps, office mugs, plastic spoons, can opener, napkins, salt and pepper, desk calendars, letter openers, staple remover, dead ball-point pens, photographs, and perhaps a petrified apple core. What you find will probably surprise you.

Pile everything in two huge piles. Put paperwork in one pile, and nonpaper items in another pile. You'll want to consider both piles. Since it's easier, take the nonpaper pile first.

Examine each nonpaper item. Ask several questions.

"Why do I have this in my desk?"
"What do I use it for?"
"How often do I use it?"
"Where should I keep it?"

Throw out anything you're not using. Don't keep something just because you have space for it. There is nothing wrong with having empty desk drawers.

Keep the frequently used items close at hand, easy to find, and quick to use. Try to use the center desk drawer for these items. If the center drawer is not big enough, then use the top drawers on either side of the center drawer.

Next, tackle the paper pile. Take each piece of paper and ask the Critical Paperwork Question: "Will I really do anything with this?" There are only three answers: yes, no, or maybe. Each answer requires a different action.

If you answer no, throw it out. There is no point in keeping something you won't do anything with.

If you answer maybe, toss it into a big box, or use one of your empty desk drawers. Keep the box in an out-of-the-way place. If you ever need anything in it, you'll know where it is.

Your "maybe box" is a temporary halfway station between your desk and your wastebasket. Use it to age only those items you really aren't sure about. Almost everything you put in it will turn out to be junk. When the box is full, dump it.

You will probably answer yes to much of your paper. But take a minute to remember the lesson of Chapter Two on the importance of goals. Remember, there are only two reasons for doing anything: if it will help you achieve your goals, or if it will help someone else achieve their goals. If it won't help either of you accomplish something worthwhile, why keep it?

If you answer yes, then ask a second question: "When will I do it?" There are only three practical answers for this question. You will

1. Do it now, today.
2. Do it one day this month.
3. Do it one month this year.

After deciding when you will handle it, you're now ready for the third question: "Where will I keep it?" Each answer to the "when" question suggests a different home for the "where" question.

If you decide to do it today, put it on top of your desk. These items need immediate action. However, since you're staying late tonight to clean up your desk, this may not be a practical answer. You probably won't be acting on most paper tonight.

Use a Tickler File

If you decide to handle it one day this month or one month this year, write the date in the upper right-hand corner. Then, file the paper in a tickler file under the appropriate date. Figure 7-1 shows a typical daily and monthly tickler file. If you're unfamiliar with the tickler file technique, you're in for a pleasant surprise.

Items to be handled one day this month are placed in the files labeled from 1 to 31. These files refer to the days of the current month. Items to be handled in later months are put in one of the files labeled from January to December.

If you don't have a tickler file, then make one. Use hanging folders, and put them in your deep desk drawer. If you don't have a deep desk drawer, use a nearby filing cabinet. Label one set of folders for every day of the month, 1 to 31. Label another set of folders for every month of the year, January to December.

Some of your paper will require only filing. Don't file it later; file it now. We'll cover filing in more detail later in this chapter.

Throw away all your pending folders, pending boxes, or pending files. Putting something into a pending file is the easiest way to forget

Figure 7-1. Daily and monthly tickler file.

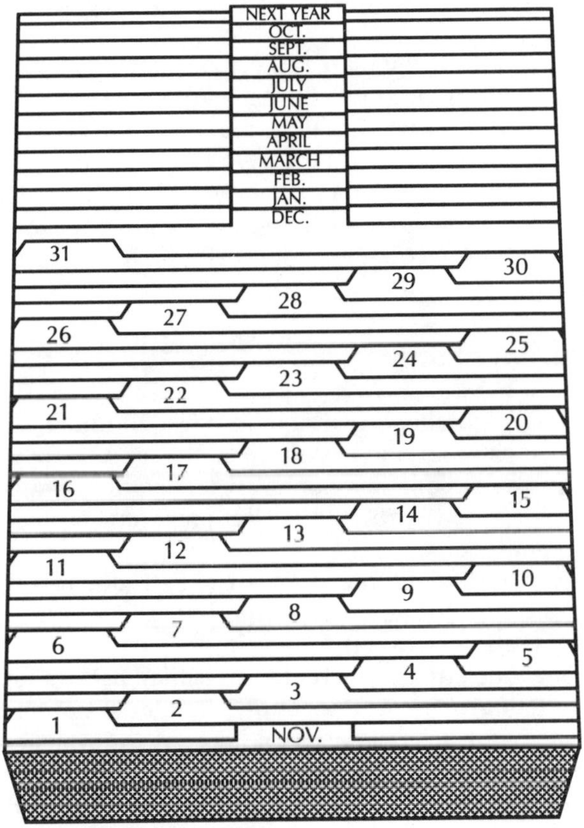

it. Out of sight, out of mind. A tickler file beats a pending file any day.

Some people try to use their calendar as a tickler system. This is risky and clumsy. For example, you receive an application for a conference to be held in six months. You don't want to send it back until four months from now, just in time to get the early registration discount. You could turn to your calendar four months from now and write a note to do this. But where will you put the registration forms? Or, suppose you make a note to mail the registration form on the 14th but something happens and you don't get to it. It's easy to flip the calendar page and forget all about the registration. A tickler file solves both these problems.

Some of us worry about whether we will find the things we put in tickler files. For example, suppose prospective clients inquire about your services. You send them the information they request. Then, you put a copy of your letter in the tickler file for follow-up in ten days. Suppose, though, that the prospect calls you again in four days. Where did you put the letter?

If you only have a few cases like this, just look through your tickler file until you find it. If you have a lot of this, however, you may want to create a cross-index. For example, one company used a two-part prospect inquiry form to do this. One copy went into the tickler file by follow-up date. The other copy was filed alphabetically in a cross-index folder. Each copy indicated the location of the other.

Use cross-index files only for critical issues. Keep them on paper or in the computer.

Use a Variation of a Tickler File

Some of the larger notebook planner/organizer products use a variation of tickler files, combined with an alphabetical cross-index for everything. Future actions are noted on the planning sheet for the specific day. The paper to go with the action is filed alphabetically at the back of the notebook.

For example, consider our conference registration form discussed earlier. We could turn to the sheet for the 14th and write:

"Mail registration form (N)."

The (N) indicates that the actual form is filed behind tab N at the back of the notebook. Then, you simply three-hole punch the registration form and put it in the alpha section of the notebook. In essence, you create an automatic cross-index file for everything.

The advantages of this system is that you have everything with you at all times. You can work wherever you are. However, if you seldom leave your office, a regular tickler file in the drawer is all you need.

Manage the Top of Your Desk

Once you get your desk cleaned up, then keep it clean. It takes more effort to keep it clean than to clean it in the first place. It is easier, however, if you keep the paper moving. Once it stops moving, clutter grows.

To keep your desk clean, concentrate on the four Ds of paperwork: dump, delegate, do, or delay. If you don't do one of the first three Ds, you will automatically get the fourth D. All you have done, however, is put off doing one of the first three Ds—and promoted clutter while delaying.

Remember that only about 20 percent of the paper crossing your desk is really worthwhile. That's what you want to do or delegate first. Eighty percent of the paper is marginal or worthless; dump it or stuff it in a "maybe drawer" and move on. Make decisions promptly, and you will delay paper less often.

Dealing With Incoming Paperwork

Whenever a piece of paper comes your way, ask yourself the following three questions:

"Will I really do anything with this?"
"When will I do it?"
"Where will I keep it?"

Saying yes to the first question is easy. Deciding when you will do it is tough. Remember, though, that you don't run out of work (paper), you run out of time.

Most of us simply assume we must do something with each piece of paper. Trouble is, we don't know when. We set it aside for when we have more time. We'll get to it as soon as we can. It's this kind of fuzzy decision making that soon buries us under a mountain of paper, much of it worthless. You're not getting anywhere, and you're feeling guilty.

Delegating paperwork to those who should handle it is also a good idea. However, in many organizations there are fewer places to delegate these days. Reorganizations, downsizing, flatter organizations, and leaner organizations mean fewer managers, fewer secretaries, and fewer support staff. In the past, lots of junk got done because we had enough staff who did it. That's no longer true. We must think more today. We must decide what really helps and what doesn't.

Consider to whom you might delegate the paper, and why they should do it. Don't delegate junk just to get rid of it. Consider when to delegate it, and how to delegate it. What will be due back to you and when? Make a note of follow-up actions and things due to you. Drop the note into your tickler file for the appropriate action date.

No one is perfect. Stacks of paper accumulate in spite of your best intentions. At the end of the day, go through the stack and ask the three questions. Make this a regular part of your process for planning tomorrow. Don't go home until you've nailed down every loose piece of paper.

Mail

If you have a secretary to open your mail, you're more fortunate than you realize. More and more people are opening their own these days, and the trend will likely continue. However, regardless of who opens the mail, the trick is to do it the smart way.

Most people think of mail as paper that comes from the post office. However, mail also includes in-company distribution, electronic mail, voice mail, faxes, Federal Express, UPS, meetings, phone calls, or even your own notes. All of these are sources of paperwork. All require decisions.

We should approach mail with a proactive strategy, seeking the golden nuggets. Instead, most of us only react to the mail, struggling to handle it all, and feeling frustrated as it piles up around us.

Just because someone sends you a piece of paper doesn't mean you have to read it, or even that you should read it. You have limited time and should handle only the mail that is important. Important mail is any that helps you achieve your goals.

Do you really throw away junk mail without opening it, or do you take a peek just out of curiosity? Many of us like to see what's inside. If you have the time, go right ahead and look. Those of us who mail lots of advertising material will love you. However, remember that an envelope never opened is paper you never have to handle. So, the first line of defense in your war against paper is to throw out as much as you can without opening it. With outside mail, this is especially easy to do.

Knowing what to open—and what to throw out unopened—is easier than you may think. There are clues all over the envelope to help you decide. For instance, look at the return address, or the lack of one. Check the postage rate. Notice how the postage is stamped. The color of the envelope, the type of envelope, the size of the envelope, and even how stuffed it is are other clues. Is the envelope addressed to you, or to someone else? Was it addressed by label, typewriter, computer, or is it handwritten? Read anything printed on the outside of the envelope. Just by paying attention to all the clues, you can probably pitch a significant percent of your mail and be done with it immediately.

You will also need a good sorting system when you start opening the mail that remains. Start with the three basic groups: action, information, reading. Add other categories as you need them. For instance, you may want to break action paper into urgent and non-urgent. You might even want to save certain types of junk mail for slow days only, or for reading as you fall asleep.

Action paper includes any paper that requires you do something. Keep it separate so you can handle it quickly. The information category is for those things you need to know daily. The reading category is for all the other material you will want to read, like magazines or reports. If there is quite a lot of reading material, you may want to sort it into more than one category. Subgroups might include magazines, newsletters, or company reports.

Sorting paper makes it easier to respond to your mail—not just a haphazard approach, but a systematic approach. Schedule time for action paper first, then information paper, and finally the other reading paper.

Here is a little-known trick you can test. You will probably make faster decisions, better decisions, and discard more mail if you stand up to open it. An excellent place may be to use the top of your filing cabinets. The added benefit is that you can file material instantly, as you open it.

Mail arouses curiosity. Whenever it arrives, we tend to drop whatever we're doing and look through the mail. The more often it arrives, the more often we interrupt and distract ourselves. With each interruption, the risk of getting sidetracked increases.

No matter how many times your mail is delivered, reserve one time a day to open it, preferably after 2:00 P.M. The later the better. When you open mail later in the day, you'll be more in charge. The earlier you open your mail, the more likely you will react to it. If possible, have the mail delivered somewhere besides your desk. If nothing else, put a box by the door, and ask them to dump your mail in the box.

Sort your mail as you open it. Never put the papers back into the envelope. File things immediately; don't put them in a to-be-filed tray. Don't set aside action paper without scheduling the first action. Ask the three questions listed earlier in this chapter. Pass along paper that belongs somewhere else.

Magazines, Books, and Tapes

Almost everyone has trouble throwing out certain kinds of paper. *National Geographic* is probably the most-saved magazine in the world. Even people who don't read it save it. And just try throwing out a book, especially a hardcover. If it's a book, we assume it must be valuable. (Of course, this book really *is* valuable!) That's also true for audiotapes, and double for videotapes. Even the most calloused discarder turns cautious when faced with books and tapes.

Books, magazines, and tapes are only ways of presenting information. There's just something about them that has a hammerlock on human emotions. How we feel about them may have nothing to do with their value. They must be evaluated like any other kind of mail.

If you can't bring yourself to trashing unwanted books or tapes, consider other actions. An alternative may be giving them to libraries, trade associations, or friends. What is unimportant for you may be very helpful for someone else.

Before reading a magazine, scan the cover and check the contents. Rip out articles of interest and throw the rest out. Carry articles with you to read in odd moments. Or read them at coffee breaks or lunch.

Before reading a book, check the contents page, look over the index and read the dustcover or preface. What do you hope to gain by reading it? Is there likely to be anything new in it? Only go for the gold.

Everyone has a pile of magazines they have been saving so they can read them later. The higher the pile, the greater the guilt and the lower the probability that any of them will get read. The best thing you can do is throw them out. Discard magazines if you haven't read them within three to five weeks. Any stack more than six inches high is too high. Throw them out. Don't worry about missing something important.

Publishers have many strategies to get you engaged in their product. Color, graphics, hardcovers, boxed sets, or slipcovers for storage all increase perceived value. Even the local newspapers are using color as never before. Perceived value, however, does not imply real value. Even a boxed set of books can be junk to you.

Don't subscribe to a magazine for more than one year. Before renewing, evaluate it. How much has it really helped? Don't renew low-value magazines; look for something better.

You might even consider dropping all your subscriptions and going to the library. You will find a wide selection of books, magazines, and newspapers, plus a reference librarian. Reference librarians are among the most knowledgeable people anywhere. They can find anything.

Storing Paper

Certain types of paper must be saved. Your accountant or lawyer can supply a retention schedule for these items. If the law says keep it, then keep it. However, there are no legal requirements for most of the paper we save.

Decide What to Keep

We often keep paper "just in case." You never know when you'll need it. And you're sure to need it just as soon as you throw it out. Unfortunately, few of us have well-thought-out criteria for what to keep and what to discard. As a result, we keep too much.

Studies show that you will only use 5 to 10 percent of the material you file. Half of your files are outdated, and half of your files are duplicates. One expert estimates that it costs about $2,000 annually to maintain every filing cabinet.

Before you file anything, ask yourself the following questions:

- Is it already outdated?
- Is it a duplicate?
- Do I really need it?
- What am I most likely to use it for?
- How often will I need it?
- Is this high-quality information?
- What's the worst thing that could happen if I didn't have this?
- Could I live without it?
- Where else could I get it?
- Am I saving it out of sentiment?

Your answers to these questions will help you decide whether or not you really should save it or file it.

Organize Your Files

Organize your files so they are quick to use. You don't want to waste time filing or retrieving information. It should only take seconds to find anything. Files may be arranged alphabetically, numerically, chronologically, or some combination of these three. For example, all client folders may be filed alphabetically, but the contents of the folder could be arranged chronologically.

Be sure to put similar things together. Nothing is more confusing than to have similar information filed in several different places. This often happens when you forget you already have a file and create a duplicate one.

Use hanging folders for greatest speed and ease. Stagger the labels for faster searching. The tickler file shown in Figure 7-1 shows a common example of staggered labels.

Files you use often should be closest to your desk. Arrange them in any order that makes sense to you. Use topical headings that match the way you think. Don't try to use someone else's set of labels. Create your own.

List the contents of each file. You could tape this to the front of each drawer, or keep it in a notebook or computer. This will help avoid duplicating a file you already have. If the list is on the drawer front, it also makes it easier to search for specific files.

Clean out your files regularly. Some people find it useful to put a self-destruct date on anything they file. If the item isn't used by that date, get rid of it. Every time you use a file, take a few seconds to remove outdated or unnecessary information.

At least once a year, go through all your files and toss out as much as you can. Many companies turn this into a fun time. They close the office and have a paper-pitching party. Everyone shows up for work in old clothes to clean out drawers, files, and closets. The company provides food and drinks. By the end of the day, there is a lot less paper in the office.

Consider using partitioned folders for project files. Partitioned files are like gluing several manila folders together. It allows you to keep various categories of paper separated and easily accessible within the same folder. Most partitioned folders have a metal clip at the top of each partition. This lets you attach papers so they don't fall out or get jumbled up. Partitioned files are now available with pockets so you can easily include things like computer floppy disks in the file folder.

At the end of a project, clean out the file. Summarize any pertinent information, and discard everything you can. This will be especially helpful for ongoing projects with revolving chairpeople. The incoming chairperson can quickly review the past without having to wade through reams of useless paper.

Color coding is another way to speed up filing procedures. Use color to highlight types of information. For instance, suppose you select blue for all your customer files. If a customer file were misfiled, it would be much faster to look for a blue folder out of place, than having to read all the various file labels.

People are born with the urge to save or throw out. Savers, of course, keep everything, both at work and at home. Some things saved at home may turn into valuable antiques or collector items. However, this is rarely true for paper saved at work.

By the way, if you use computers a lot, you probably have a lot of junk stored on your hard disk, or sitting around in all those floppies. It's a good idea to set aside time at least once a year to clean out the computer too.

Streamlining Paper

The trick with paper is to keep it moving. Paper stops when you fail to decide and act promptly. Once stopped, it tends to root and multiply. To keep your paper moving, here are some quick tips that may help.

Everyone has heard the advice "Handle your paper once." This means do what must be done the first time you pick it up. File it, answer it, discard it, pass it on to someone else. Make notes on the bottom of a letter or memo and send it along. Put things in the file, don't pile it to be filed later. Route things to the proper person. Decide on action dates and drop it in your tickler file.

The following suggestions can also help you stay on top of paperwork.

1. *Dictate responses to letters as soon as you read them.* Eighty percent of the time you know exactly what must be said. You don't have to think about it or check anything out with someone else. Dictate it or keyboard it immediately. Don't set it aside for later; do it now.

2. *Experiment and test your paperwork.* You can probably dispense with 50 to 90 percent of your mail right on the spot as you open it.

3. *Dictate key thoughts only.* Let your secretary compose the copy. If necessary, you can review or revise it before the final printing. And do the revising on-screen. Don't waste time printing rough drafts. How you handle paperwork determines how long it takes. The data in the following list compare four common methods for generating finished copy:*

Handwritten:	10–15 words per minute
Dictated to secretary:	20–30 words per minute
Dictated by machine:	60–80 words per minute
Typed or keyboarded:	20–50 words per minute

4. *Set deadlines for yourself.* Learn to work faster. Try to finish within the allotted time.

5. *Forget about perfection.* It takes only 10 to 20 percent as much time to do an adequate job as it takes to do a "perfect" job. That's not to say you should do sloppy work; just don't waste time trying to be unnecessarily "perfect."

6. *Schedule a specific time for doing paperwork.* If possible, do it in a specific place. Doing a task at the same time and place every day develops both mental and physical habit patterns. It's easier to concentrate and do a better job in less time.

7. *Act right away.* Never set aside a piece of action paper without taking some action on it. This prevents it from being lost or forgotten.

*Based on material from Dartnell Research Institute, Chicago.

At the very least, decide when to take the next action, and put it in your tickler file.

8. *Develop routine procedures and standard responses.* Many companies have standard letters in the computer. Just match the letter to the circumstance. There is no need to keep generating the same routine responses.

9. *Analyze your paperwork and review your procedures regularly.* A State of Indiana study showed that removing one line from a form could save three to five minutes of processing time. That could amount to thousands of hours every year. Remember *kaizen* (see Chapter Four): Continual incremental improvements yield big dividends.

10. *Stand up to work.* Get a stand-up desk, or raise your work counter. Standing up is usually faster and often less fatiguing.

11. *Look for ideas.* Look for any tool or technique that will help you streamline paperwork. Browse through the large office products catalog. Visit a well-stocked office supply store. Go visit other offices and see what they have done.

12. *Stay updated on new technology.* For example, electronic mail, voice mail, and fax can cut hours from your paperwork chores. Dragon Systems, Inc. (90 Bridge St., Newton, MA 02158, Tel: 617-965-5200) recently perfected a computer software program that lets you talk directly to the computer, with no need for anyone to intervene. Other programs are bound to emerge soon.

13. *Buy the best chair you can afford.* Top-of-the-line ergonomic chairs will keep you relaxed and refreshed all day. A bad chair compounds fatigue and muscle problems. If you have a choice, economize on the desk, and buy an excellent chair.

14. *Finally, don't make copies unless you really need them.* About half of all paper filed are duplicate copies.

Staying Up-to-Date

Truth is, no one can read everything, although many are still trying. They indiscriminately try to read every paper, report, memo, magazine, and newspaper crossing their desk. They don't know how to separate value from junk, and they worry that they'll miss something important. Ironically, they do miss important things because they spend so much time perusing junk.

Learn to Read Faster

Learning to read faster is a good idea. Most adults read an average of only 200 to 250 words per minute. You can double your average reading speed in thirty days by practicing only ten minutes daily. You can attend classes or buy self-study courses on audio or video cassettes. Believe it or not, you can even read a book to learn how to read faster.

With only a little effort, you can triple or even quadruple your reading speed. That would mean less time to read what you've been reading. Or, it could mean reading even more in the same amount of time you've been spending. You win either way.

On the other hand, you don't have to read everything yourself. Try to share the reading with others. For example, suppose several people need to read the same material. Groups of three or four could divide the total, with each person reading a portion. Once a week, they could share the highlights of key parts of what they've each read. Sharing could be done over lunch, through electronic mail, voice mail, or fax.

Bunching reading material is another good way to get through material faster. Instead of allowing twenty minutes to read a magazine, try to go through six magazines in the same twenty minutes. This forces you to skip over all the trivia and focus only on articles that are relevant for you. This is another example of Parkinson's law: Work expands to fill the time available. Remove the slack time, and you'll focus on real value faster.

Use Summaries

Use summaries whenever you can. Executive Soundview Book Summaries (Tel: 1-800-521-1227) publishes excellent summaries of current business books. It does a superb job. Fast Track (Tel: 1-800-274-1996) summarizes business books on audiotapes. Newstrack (Tel: 1-800-776-5771) issues a monthly cassette tape summarizing the top articles from 100 business magazines. There are probably many others we don't know about, and there will undoubtedly be new ones. Staying up-to-date is a massive problem, and it is getting more difficult all the time.

You could also create your own summaries. The engineering division of one firm did this. Their engineers were having trouble finding time to read all the technical journals. The company hired one of their recently retired engineers to read all the journals. He then prepared a short summary of the key information for the other engineers. The summaries required much less reading time. We also suggested that the company record the summaries on cassette tapes. This allowed the engineers to get the same technical updates while commuting to work. They no longer needed to look for so much reading time.

Listen to Tapes

We all need information, but reading is only one way to get it. Putting information on tape makes a lot of sense. The average American spends at least two hours commuting every day. Many people listen to tapes while they exercise. Recording information allows people to listen even when they can't read. Plus, some people would rather listen than read.

With information on tape, you can also speed up the listening rate. The VSC Corporation patented a process for speeding up playback speed and also adjusting the pitch to avoid the chipmunk effect. With their process you can double your listening rate. Doubling the playback speed is well within the listening capacity of adults. The average adult could then hear material even faster than he could read it. The following list shows the comparative rates of reading, speaking, and listening for average adults:

Reading:	200–250 words per minute
Speaking:	80–150 words per minute
Listening:	300–500 words per minute

Several companies produce fast-playback recorders under license from VSC Corporation. One example is Radio Shack, Model 14-1052. Drop by your nearest Radio Shack store, and try it out. You'll be amazed at how easy it is to hear and understand tapes at twice their recorded speed.

More companies should be using tape to distribute information. At least give people the option of reading or listening. This would allow for both greater flexibility and personal preference. Some of us would even be able to listen faster than we can read.

Producing Less Paperwork

Write less, say more. Poor writing compounds reading problems. Experts estimate that most adults write three to five times more words than they need to convey their message. This means that the reader must plow through three to five times more material.

We've learned to be poor writers; it's time to become better writers. If we wrote fewer words, there would be less reading. Eliminate unnecessary words, sentences, and paragraphs. Take a writing seminar. Study Strunk and White's little book, *The Elements of Style* (Third Edition, New York: Macmillan, 1979). It's the best eighty-five pages ever written on how to be a better writer. Practice their suggestions. It will take a little more work in the beginning, but it will eventually save a lot of time for both you and your readers.

We can't manage our time if we can't manage our paper, so it's time to conquer our paper enemy. Here is an excellent place to practice *kaizen*. Challenge every sheet. How could it be improved, shortened, or eliminated? We can no longer assume that somehow we'll find time to get it all done. We won't. The alternative to an aggressive attack on paperwork is to continued being buried under the avalanche.

Technology alone will not solve the paperwork problem. Since 1957, we've heard that the computer will make paper obsolete. Don't believe it. Computers create more paper, not less. Technology often creates a useful tool—and sometimes a cruel tyrant.

Too many of us continue to operate with the same assumptions and personal skills that worked okay in the past. Today, though, they must be replaced. Paperwork is growing geometrically. If you can barely keep up with it today, you won't have a chance tomorrow. Two things must change. First, we must change our attitudes and assumptions. We must think information, not paper. We need to move past the management paranoia that requires paper documentation for everything and stifles performance.

Second, we need to master new skills, like dictating machines, computers, and cellular telephones. Electronics are here to stay, whether we like it or not. You can't lick them, and the faster you join them the more you'll benefit.

Third, we need to drastically improve our organizational systems. Search out and remove bottlenecks. Streamline your operations. Shorten decision loops. Do anything you can to lessen the paperwork burden on people so they can produce more real results.

Scoring Guide for Chapter Seven Quiz				
SA	**MA**	**U**	**MD**	**SD**
1. 5	4	3	2	1
2. 5	4	3	2	1
3. 5	4	3	2	1
4. 1	2	3	4	5

Eight
Minimizing
Interruptions

The only problem with this job is people.

Anonymous

Before reading this chapter, please circle your response to each of the following statements. A scoring guide is at the end of the chapter.

SA = Strongly Agree   **MA** = Mildly Agree   **U** = Undecided
MD = Mildly Disagree   **SD** = Strongly Disagree

							Score
1.	I analyze my interruptions and systematically work on reducing or eliminating them.	SA	MA	U	MD	SD	_____
2.	I usually bunch items together and handle several things in one visit or call, so I won't interrupt others so much during the day.	SA	MA	U	MD	SD	_____
3.	Distractions and socializing often keep me from concentrating on my work.	SA	MA	U	MD	SD	_____
4.	Interruptions are a big problem in my job.	SA	MA	U	MD	SD	_____
						Total Score	_____

"Hi, there! Gotta minute?" How many times have you heard this? Trouble is, this "minute" will probably last at least twenty minutes. Whether telephone calls or drop-in visitors, interruptions will take up a sizable portion of your day. In offices, for example, you will probably be interrupted every 6 to 8 minutes. Some interruptions are positive, some are negative. Some are worthwhile, some aren't. Some are controllable, some aren't.

Attitude

Realize that interruptions are part of your job, and it may be your attitude that needs adjusting. When interrupted, most of us are at least mildly irritated; we don't like to stop what we're doing and focus on something else. Sincerely try to look at the interruption in a different way. Instead of being upset when an interruption occurs, think of it simply as part of the job. You'll be less frustrated and better able to stay in control of the situation.

Realize, too, though, that you will not achieve total control of interruptions. When you work with people, you must resign yourself to their unpredictable actions. The basic idea is to accept the noncontrollable and control the controllable. The key is to allow enough time in your schedule for unexpected, uncontrollable events. If you allow flexibility for interruptions, you won't be so frustrated when they do occur. If you don't allow adequate flexibility in your schedule, the interruptions will occur anyway, and your frustrations will soar.

Analyze Interruptions

Unfortunately, most of us only complain about their interruption problems. Only a few systematically analyze them and work to eliminate, reduce, or control them. Even a little constructive action is better than years of complaining.

The single most useful approach for reducing interruptions is to keep records. Note who interrupts you, when they interrupt, how long it takes and what it is about. By studying this record you can learn a great deal about your interruption patterns. The Interruption Log and Telephone Log shown in Chapter Four (Figure 4-4) are excellent tools to help you collect data on interruptions.

Chances are, you will find that most of your interruptions come from those who are closest to you. These are the people who talk to you most often. Your records will probably show that most of the contacts concern routine or trivial issues. Only a few are critically important.

Look for patterns among your interruptions. Are there a few people who interrupt you constantly? Do some issues generate far more interruptions than others? Are telephone calls a bigger problem than drop-in visitors? Are mornings better or worse than afternoons? How many of your calls are to the wrong number? How many interruptions concern social matters instead of work? No matter what the pattern, knowing what it is puts you way ahead. You can't solve a problem until you have accurately identified it.

Everyone struggles with interruptions. Most of us constantly complain about them, but do little else. It would be far better to analyze them and to work systematically at reducing them. In the words of the ancient Greek philosophers, "It is better to light one candle than curse the darkness."

Keep It Brief

You can't prevent all the interruptions. However, you can often control how long they last. If you can keep them short, you will solve half the problem.

For example, a recent study reported that the average unplanned telephone call takes almost eleven minutes. The average planned call lasts only about seven minutes. Planning telephone calls would obviously help both parties.

Consider how to greet callers. "Hi, Tom! How are you?" is an open invitation to visit. Your caller might even feel obligated to respond with small talk. However, the caller is more likely to get right to the point if you say, "Hi, Tom! How can I help you?"

There is a time for socializing and a time for not socializing. Over half the conversation in business calls is not about business. Stay focused on the reason for the call.

Reorganize your work, or the timing of your tasks. For instance, most people go to lunch at the same time: noon. If you were to work during the normal lunch hour, you would probably have very few interruptions. Another possibility is the first hour of the day. Try to concentrate on your important work while most people are occupied with coffee, conversation, and newspapers during this time. Most interruption patterns don't build up until after 9:00 or 9:30 A.M.

Tell visitors you only have a few minutes. Gently encourage them to get to the point quickly. Keep a large clock close by. Glance at the clock from time to time. Or use a timer to remind yourself to keep conversations short. The more people are aware of time, the less time they waste.

Train people to do their thinking before they come talk to you. Ask them to write down exactly what they want you to do. Frequently, they will solve their own problems as they think about them. At the very least, your time together will be shorter and more productive because of their being prepared.

Go to other people's offices when they need to see you. It makes them feel good and gives you more control. It's usually easier to leave someone else's office than it is to get people out of your office.

Finally, be creative. Several years ago, a client showed us an excellent example of how to keep interruptions short. He had cut two inches off the front legs of his visitors' chairs.

Stand Up

When someone drops in to see you, don't remain sitting at your desk. Stand up, look them in the eye, and ask, "How can I help you?" Unless the visit requires sitting, remain standing while you talk.

Most of us sit when we go to talk to others. Think about it. What might happen if you would stand up when someone drops in to see you? If you don't sit down, they probably won't sit either. It would be a breech of good etiquette. They will probably get to the point quicker and be on their way sooner. Then, you can sit down and get back to your own work.

Standing might even improve your relationships with others. Here is a common example. Someone pops into your office. You don't even stop writing, or lift your eyes off whatever you are doing. Yet, you tell them to go ahead, you are listening. Do you ever think about the message you have just telegraphed to the other person? If you would stand up when they enter, you would automatically given them your full attention. The nonverbal message you send would be much more positive, in addition to saving time.

Bunch Things Together

Most of us interrupt others in a haphazard manner. We call them or drop in on them whenever we think of it. Our focus is largely on what we are doing, what we need, what we are trying to avoid. We seldom stop to think much about what this constant barrage does to others. However, we often complain about what their constant interruptions do to us.

Some of the interruptions are important, but most are merely routine. In fact, most interruptions are less important than the work they interrupt. Timing is not critical for most routine matters. Therefore, you could bunch several of these routine matters together and handle them all at one time.

You may find that the fast pace of your job helps create constant interruptions. For example, suppose your job involves many projects. You are in and out of the office often. People never know for sure when they can count on seeing you. Even when you are in, you're always busy. So, they begin to catch you whenever they can. Every time they think of something, they call you or pop into your office. After a while, this becomes their regular habit for contacting you.

To get better results, ask people to hold all the routine items and go over them at one time. Bunch your routine items too. Schedule regular meetings with key people. Encourage people to set appointments instead of relying so much on spontaneous drop-in visits. Just a simple one-on-one meeting, once a day or once a week, could work miracles in your schedule.

To help bunch items together, you can keep a notebook, one page per name. You can write topics to discuss on the pages. Periodically, call or meet with each person to go over the accumulated items. One good technique is to write your question or comment on the left side of the page. Then, use the right side of the page to note the replies.

You may prefer to collect items in file folders, boxes, trays, or even wall pocket files. One creative person used a white board and marker pens. He divided the board into several grids and assigned one name per grid. He made notes in the grids. When he called to discuss the items, he erased them as they were covered. When he had erased all the items, he said good-bye. Instead of a white board, you could use a bulletin board. Thumbtacks or push pins could hold notes under different groups.

Whichever way you do it, bunching items together is a great idea. Start with yourself and then try to convince others to do it too. If everyone were to bunch routine interruptions, half our interruption problems would disappear overnight.

Rethink Your Open-Door Policy

Many companies promote open-door policies to encourage the flow of ideas and information. Often, though, the open-door policy produces more problems than benefits. In most cases it simply means that you are at the beck and call of anyone at any time. To allow others to control arbitrarily your time all day is nonsense.

The philosophy underlying open-door policies means that people should be easily accessible to others. This does not preclude structuring the day and scheduling contact time. To get the best results, everyone needs some "time off" when they can concentrate without interruption. Go back and review our discussion of quiet time in Chapter Six.

Communicate Effectively

Proper communication is essential if we wish to reduce interruptions. Hasty instructions or explanations often cause interruptions as people seek clarification. Take time to do it right, especially when dealing with new or unfamiliar projects. People are reluctant to admit that they didn't understand, so you must take the time to make sure they did. Lack of understanding creates all kinds of problems, as well as more interruptions.

One way to guard against miscommunication is to restate your idea in several ways until you are certain it is clear. Or you might ask others to restate the idea in their own words. It may also be a good idea to follow up with a written confirmation.

Remember too that nonverbal communication is a significant part of your message. Your gait, expression, dress, movements, and general attitude all affect any message you present. Try to make the verbal and nonverbal parts consistent with each other.

However, effective communication is not achieved overnight. There must be trust within the work group. People must feel free to exchange ideas, disagree, and risk mistakes. Only then will they be truly receptive to your messages.

Taming the Telephones

Telephones are important. Everyone knows that. But they can also be a waste of time. It depends on how you use them. For example, the average manager spends between two and three hours on the telephone every day. Studies show, however, that about half of all business calls aren't about business. Even calls that start discussing worthwhile topics often deteriorate into trivia. Poorly conducted conversations don't accomplish much.

Plan your calls before you dial. As mentioned earlier, one study found that the average business call was almost eleven minutes. However, the average planned call was only seven minutes. Planning will make your calls far more productive. It will also make your calls shorter.

To plan your calls, ask yourself why you are calling. What result do you intend to achieve? After you clarify your purpose, consider how to accomplish it. How should you say it? What words should you use? What sequence or structure to use? How should you position your points or phrase your questions?

Also consider how much time you will need. Most of us are short of time. If you need more than a few minutes, you may want to arrange a telephone appointment. Telephone appointments aren't as common as face-to-face appointments, but for time-conscious people they make a lot of sense.

Give careful thought to your opening remarks. Realize that whenever you make an unexpected call, you are creating an interruption for the other person. Most of us at least mildly resent interruptions. The mere fact that the phone rings is an irritation. Many people are not in a positive frame of mind as they answer the phone. At the very least, they weren't thinking about you or why you are calling. For goodness' sake, don't waste their time chatting about the weather. Get right to the point.

Ask people you call often when they are most likely to be in, and call at these times. Tell them the best time to call you too. Using preferred call times can help reduce telephone tag.

Always give complete information. "Hello. This is Merrill Douglass. I'm calling Fred Anderson about our pending contract. Will you please connect us?" This not only saves time spent on the inevitable questions but will also get you connected more often.

Skip the small talk. Remember, telephone calls are interruptions. While you're asking "How are you?" they're wondering what you want. Getting right to the point will save time for both of you.

Close calls promptly. If the other party seems to be drifting, serve notice that you are ready to hang up. "Before we hang up, Chris, I'd like to review what I need to deliver to you" is a tactful way to indicate that you're finished with the conversation.

Consider alternatives. AT&T recently reported that the chances are only one in six that you will reach the person you're calling on the first try. It might be better to send a postcard, letter, electronic note, or fax.

Keep records of incoming calls. Find out who calls, when, about what. Analyze this record to determine who should answer your telephone. Generally speaking, the higher your organizational level, the greater the risk that answering your own phone is a time waster.

Train people to answer telephones effectively. Consider what they should say and how they should say it. Which questions should they ask? What information will you need to act on the call or delegate it to someone else? When and how should callers be referred to others?

Trim Telephone Tag

Part of your phone time is spent playing telephone tag. Someone calls when you're out and leaves a message. When you return the call, the person's gone, so you leave a message. Then the person calls again, and you call again, and round and round it goes. Telephone tag is frustrating. According to one study, you could waste over two years of your life just playing telephone tag. Here are five tips to help you reduce the problem.

1. Ask people you call frequently when they prefer to get calls or when you can most likely reach them by telephone. Try to call them at those times. Tell them when your preferred call time is or when they are most likely to reach you by telephone.

2. If the person you are calling is not available, ask if another person can help you. You may find that someone else can help you even faster and better than the person you were trying to reach.

3. Rather than leaving a message that you called, you may prefer to call again. If you reach a secretary, ask when the person is most likely to return. Ask what time would be best to call. Maybe you can even set up an appointment for a telephone meeting.

4. If you must leave a message, be sure it's a complete message. An AT&T study showed that 97 percent of messages contained only a name and a number. Leaving a complete message increases your chances for a successful result. Tell the party you are trying to reach who you are, why you are calling, where you can be reached, and what time is best to return your call. Be sure to include anything else the other person will need in order to help you. However, with a complete message, the other person has more options for helping you, even if a different person calls back. If nothing else, the return caller can leave the answer on your machine if you're not there.

5. Finally, look for alternative ways to contact people. Many people are finding that fax machines, electronic mail, voice mail, or cellular phones all help reduce the telephone-tag problem. Many people have concluded their business simply by leaving messages on each other's answering machines.

Socializing

Socializing is like aspirin: A little helps a lot but too much can be deadly. The most oppressive office we've ever seen had strict rules against employees talking among themselves at any time. On the other hand, we've been in offices where people have trouble getting anything done because of all the social chatter. We need to talk to one another. Communication is the organizational grease that keeps everything working smoothly. The issue is more a matter of degree.

We want to continue the necessary socializing and stop the unnecessary part. Unnecessary socializing may stem from habit, ego,
curiosity, the desire to be liked, or even from procrastination. We've
noticed that when people don't want to do a particular job, they are
most likely to talk to someone else, either in person or on the phone.
Learn to recognize your actions for what they are. Socializing can be
reduced without your becoming antisocial.

Skip much of the social small talk. Never discuss the weather.
Most people are bored by the weather, yet they talk about it at least
ten times a day. It always snows during the winter in Michigan. It's
always hot during the summer in Atlanta. Nothing's new. Small talk
sometimes has a purpose, but don't rationalize that it's always useful.

Sometimes a caller will go on, and on, and on—saying nothing.
You might tell long-winded callers that you have another call, appointment, or emergency. Or, as a last resort, hang up . . . while *you*
are talking. Conversations seldom call for such drastic action; for most
people subtle hints are enough.

Unnecessary socializing often results from casual contacts. The
other person may not even be looking for you. In cases like this, it
would help to rearrange your furniture so you don't face the door. If
people passing by can easily see your face, they are more likely to
stop and visit.

Carefully consider the flow of work and people when designing
your office. Poor designs create problems. Items like coffee pots and
copy machines seem to attract people. If you have to wait, conversations are inevitable. Try to put them out of the way where they will
do minimal damage. It's hard to get much work done when there is a
minor convention meeting around the coffee pot next to your desk.

Distractions

Most offices are full of distractions: phones ringing, people talking,
people coming and going, clattering printers, radio stations you don't
like, boring background music, construction noise, and who knows
what else. How can you concentrate with all this happening? The
following guidelines may help you conquer noise.

1. *Reduce the noise levels.* For instance, lower the volume on the
phones. You might consider shutting off the ring completely. Blinking
lights often work as well as a bell or buzzer. Use features like call
forwarding to kick in on the first ring.

2. *Look for ways to reduce the volume on anything that produces a
noise.* Put covers on dot matrix printers or replace them with quieter

laser printers. Put copiers in separate rooms, and close the door. Remove all radios, stereos, or televisions. Replace the ballast in the fluorescent lights if they are buzzing loudly.

3. *Use white noise in the background.* White-noise machines generate sounds at wavelengths that effectively mask many ordinary office noises. Most people won't even realize it exists, yet it will effectively cover over many distracting sounds.

4. *Put sound-absorbing materials on the walls.* Visit any up-to-date radio station or recording studio to see the variety of materials available.

5. *Try wearing earphones, the bigger the better.* Even sucking on hard candy or lozenges can help you block out distractions.

6. *Place coffee machines or water fountains as far as possible from where people are working.* Put rugs or carpets on the floor. Ask people to wear soft-soled shoes.

7. *Train yourself to ignore nearby conversations.* Don't look out the window. Angle the blinds up, or pull the drapes. Rearrange your office furniture. If necessary, find places to hide when you desperately need quiet time.

8. *Analyze your floor plan.* Arrange it so people who need to interact often are close together. This not only saves time for the people involved but also cuts down on the distractions and interruptions for others.

9. *Brainstorm.* Get your office staff together and ask them to brainstorm the distraction problem. When people brainstorm a problem, they almost always come up with many ideas. Some of those ideas will probably work well.

10. *Stop procrastinating mentally.* If you are dragging your feet on some project, you will be looking for something to interrupt you, and anything will work. The more you get involved with your work, the less you'll notice many of the distractions around you. Recognize your own part in the interruptions battle, and you'll be headed down the road to success.

Remember That Interruptions Are People

As long as we work together there will be interruptions. While we can't control everything that happens during the day, we can control our response to what happens. Our responses, in turn, determine much of the impact from the events in our day.

Interruptions are part of modern corporate life. They're part of your job, but that doesn't mean you must be at the mercy of whatever interruptions occur. You can improve conditions. You can't control everything, but you probably can control more than you realize.

Interruptions are people. Remember to be gracious with people—but firm with time. You don't have to be rude. Practice prevention and reduction techniques whenever you can. Above all, practice the golden rule. Treat others as you would like to be treated. The results are terrific.

Scoring Guide for Chapter Eight Quiz				
SA	**MA**	**U**	**MD**	**SD**
1. 5	4	3	2	1
2. 5	4	3	2	1
3. 1	2	3	4	5
4. 1	2	3	4	5

Nine
Managing Travel Time

It is not worth while to go around the world to count the cats in Zanzibar.

Henry David Thoreau

Before reading this chapter, please circle your response to each of the following statements. A scoring guide is at the end of the chapter.

SA = Strongly Agree   MA = Mildly Agree   U = Undecided
MD = Mildly Disagree   SD = Strongly Disagree

							SCORE
1.	It's hard to manage time well on a business trip.	SA	MA	U	MD	SD	_____
2.	I carefully plan my business trips and never travel without a specific purpose.	SA	MA	U	MD	SD	_____
3.	I tend to eat more and drink more when I'm on business trips.	SA	MA	U	MD	SD	_____
4.	I try to finish all the paperwork from the trip before I get back to the office.	SA	MA	U	MD	SD	_____

Total Score _____

Effective time management is a popular topic of conversation these days as more and more people strive to make each day and each moment count. Successful people know where their time goes, know how to plan their time, and know the value of careful scheduling. Their office time is organized, and they are happily on their way to accomplishing important goals. Then they go on a trip.

Business people repeatedly complain that trips out of the office break down useful time-management habits they have developed. Many report that they have to spend too much time getting ready, that the trip is an unpredictable mixture of joys and woes, and that they have too much work as well as an emotional letdown when they return.

Certainly, an out-of-town trip presents more of a challenge than the routine of office life. It can, however, become a stimulating diversion and a gift of time rather than an obstacle to effective time management.

Planning Ahead

The key to a successful business trip lies in handling all the details of the trip before you leave. You want to eliminate as much uncertainty as possible so you can cut down on time-wasting hassles. Each trip should be a lesson on how you can eliminate unnecessary steps from an activity that usually takes a high toll on your time and stamina.

Must You Go?

First of all, ask yourself the following questions: Is this trip really necessary? Must I be there in person? What purpose does my physical presence serve? Could I handle the business as well by mail or phone? What about a video conference? Is there another person from my company who is in closer proximity than I? If not, is there someone else in my office who would profit from making the trip in my stead? Remember, you can delegate out-of-town tasks as well as in-house assignments.

If you make frequent trips to a particular location, perhaps you can cut down on the total number of trips. Is there a way you can do more on the trips so you won't have to travel there so often?

You might also consider asking your client to visit you. This approach will not always work, but the effort is well worth it. Your associate might just jump at the opportunity to get away for a while. For some people, particularly those who do not travel frequently, a trip is a welcome break.

Should You Fly?

When you must go yourself, be certain that you plan your trip carefully to make sure it is successful. Begin with a good travel agent. Try several agencies until you find one you like. Then stick with it. If you stay with the same travel agent, you will have someone who knows your needs, likes, and dislikes. The agent can make all the arrangements for your arrival and departure time, gather your tickets, arrange for ground transportation, and route you the way you prefer to travel. Also, if you stay with one agent, he or she will be more concerned with pleasing you than with making a sale.

Instead of automatically requesting a plane reservation each time you travel, consider other forms of transportation. Often it is simpler to drive a distance of less than 200 miles than to take a plane. When you drive, you do not have to worry about how you will get from the airport to your final destination. You avoid ticket lines, waiting rooms, flight delays, airline food, and baggage areas.

Remember too that driving time need not be wasted time. There are many things you can do while driving. Listening to tapes is an excellent activity. Many tapes on personal development, selling, languages, and time management are now available. If you get into the habit of driving, you might also consider having reports from subordinates put on tape for your review. Many of your people may even prefer this technique of reporting.

You can also make recordings while you drive. With today's portable dictating machines you can dictate correspondence, articles, and letters while you travel. You can also use these handy machines to record any important ideas that come to your mind as you drive for your secretary to transcribe later.

When you drive, you are free to refresh yourself at your leisure. Numerous rest stops are inviting, and local restaurants provide a wider selection of foods than airlines do. You can engage in isometric exercises while driving—or pull off to the side for your daily jog if the spirit moves you.

You might also consider employing a driver on a part-time basis. College students are an excellent resource. They often need the extra money and enjoy a chance to get away from their routine. Employing your own chauffeur offers you convenience, privacy, and freedom.

A car is not the only alternative to air travel. Trains also offer certain advantages when time is not crucial. You can get up and move about freely. A train is much less confining than a plane, and you can enjoy the scenery when you take a break from your labors.

If You Fly

Of course, the large majority of business executives will continue to travel by plane. The airlines are making a continued effort to improve air travel for their clientele. Here are some tips for making your plane trip more comfortable and pleasurable.

1. *Try not to fly at peak traveling times.* Holidays always bring on an extra number of tourists. More mix-ups, lost luggage, and ticketing inaccuracies take place as the volume of people increases. Fly at off-times whenever possible. Friday and Sunday nights are always busy. Commuter flights are also busy between 5:00 and 7:00 P.M. You will save a great deal of aggravation if you book less crowded flights.

2. *Book your flight early.* As soon as you know you will be taking a trip, have your travel agent make your reservation. If possible, take care of your other reservations as well—such as seat selection (when available), car rental, hotel accommodations, prepaid tickets, diet or special foods, and any other requirements you wish. If you book early, you have a better chance of getting a more direct flight to your location. The fewer connections, the lower the chances of delays, mishaps, and lost luggage. Have your agent check for any recent changes in schedules a few days before your departure. Airline flights and departure times undergo thousands of changes every month. An alert travel agent can save you hours of grief.

Check Your Reservations and Review Your Needs

Your secretary can also help you save time and energy. A few days before takeoff, your secretary should verify all appointments you have made at your destination and, whenever possible, double-check the times and locations for the various meetings you will attend so you and your associates can coordinate your schedules.

Your secretary should also make certain that your hotel reservations are confirmed and double-check any arrangements made by a travel agent or client. The room reservation is one of the most crucial concerns of any traveler. Nothing is worse than a hard day's travel followed by a "no vacancy" sign.

Developing regular checklist procedures such as the following also helps:

☐ Do I have my tickets with the other materials? Are they correct? Will I be arriving early enough to get to my meeting?

☐ Are all my materials ready to go? Do I need copies of handouts for distribution? A report to review? Are there background materials I should read? Could my secretary summarize them instead? Will the audiovisual equipment I need be ready for me in the meeting room? Do I have notepaper, calling cards, and a detailed outline of my expected performance?

☐ Do I have cash as well as credit cards? (Credit cards are a boon to travelers, but there are still times when there is no substitute for cash. You should have enough for taxi fares, tips, sundries, and emergency cash—just in case.)

☐ Will I need any secretarial services at my out-of-town destination? (Your secretary should arrange for such services beforehand so the help you need will be there to serve you.)

☐ Does my secretary have a copy of my reservations as well as phone numbers, fax numbers, and addresses where I can be reached? Have I planned to check in with my home office at a regular time at least once a day?

☐ Does my secretary know of all pending matters around the office that may require action? What action should my secretary take in my absence?

There will, of course, be certain tasks that only you can do. Review your schedule for appropriate clothes. Check the climate at your destination. Pack enough clothing but guard against excess. Too many clothes are simply confusing. Shoes and clothing should be comfortable and should not distract from the business at hand. Coordinate your wardrobe around one or two compatible colors with interchangeable parts for travel, business, and daytime or evening occasions. Style your hair simply so that it needs a minimum of attention as well as minimum of appliances.

For a one- or two-night trip, one medium piece of luggage is generally sufficient. In some instances you can fit all you need into a large attaché case. You can carry the case on the plane, thus avoiding the crowds and delays at the baggage-claims area.

If your trip takes you across more than three time zones, make special provisions for jet lag. Whenever possible, allow an extra day at your destination so that your body time can catch up with actual time. A good way to prevent jet lag is to go to sleep either a couple of hours earlier (when traveling east) or a couple of hours later (when traveling west) for a few nights before your trip. Most people experience more difficulty crossing time zones from west to east than east to west. The greater the number of time zones crossed, the more severe the problem. Learn to recognize your limit, and plan accordingly.

On departure day, collect your materials, your suitcase, your briefcase, and your tickets. Kiss your spouse and kids good-bye in time to get to the airport for a comfortable check-in. Relax a little before boarding the plane.

Pack Light

Have you ever made the mistake of packing too much for a trip? You can't help but feel sorry for the people you see struggling with several suitcases through the airport. Frequent travelers quickly learn to pack light.

1. *Start with a checklist.* A good plan will help you minimize everything. Think carefully about whether or not you will need a specific item.

2. *Plan a one-color look.* You will need fewer bulky accessories such as shoes or purses.

3. *Select double-duty clothes.* You will need fewer clothes that way, yet you will still have ample flexibility.

4. *Try to never check your luggage.* This will help force you to become more judicious about what to take with you.

5. *Miniaturize everything you can.* This is one of the big secrets for packing light. You can get miniature versions of toothpaste, shampoo, hair conditioner, razors, slippers, steam iron, hair dryer, umbrella, pants hangers, clock radio, calculator, brushes, cassette player, and dictating machine. Constantly look for ways to save space in your suitcase.

6. *Don't take with you what you can easily buy there.* For example, take your camera, but buy your extra film as you go. Take only one or two changes of clothes, and use hotel laundry services. One traveler we met took only one change of clothes on a European trip of several weeks. When his clothes were soiled, he would mail them home and buy new clothes. While we were lugging around two big suitcases, he was making do quite nicely with a lightweight duffle bag.

Making the Most of Traveling Time

A year or so ago we were waiting in one of the public lounges of the Los Angeles International Airport. Our curiosity was aroused by a distinguished gentleman carrying a large sack. We watched with interest as the man sat down on a chair, put his briefcase and coat beside him, and emptied the sack on the next seat.

Right there in the middle of the airport was a pile of mail. Magazines, letters, flyers, large manila envelopes—the works. He picked up the mail one piece at a time, glanced at it, made a note on some pieces and stuck them in his briefcase, and threw other pieces back in the sack. As our curiosity grew, we approached the man and asked him about what he was doing.

"I always save up my mail and take it with me on trips," he said. "I go through a whole month's worth at a time. It's my trip activity. It's a good idea; I don't have to bother with it at my office! Besides, there are no interruptions, and I can take my time."

We would hardly recommend that time-conscious travelers drag a month's worth of mail with them on a trip. We do have to give the man credit, though; he was certainly using his travel time! Many people waste valuable work time while they are traveling.

Work During Your Trip

Travel time can be as productive as time in the office—if you plan for it. The secret is expectations—what you expect to accomplish while on the trip. Analyze the free time you will have on the trip, and plan accordingly. This is a crucial activity if you hope to get something done while traveling. Many people who faithfully develop a daily to-do list at the office fail to practice this good habit when they are away. A to-do list is important in or out of the office. If you expect to get something accomplished when you travel, write down your expectations, and take along the necessary materials.

The amount of work you want to accomplish on a trip is directly related to how much you travel. If you travel only once or twice a year, you will probably prefer to combine more pleasure than work with your business. An occasional trip away from the office is a welcome break from the routine, so go ahead and enjoy yourself! If you travel a great deal, though, travel soon loses its thrill. You grin weakly as others comment about your jet-set life and think to yourself, "If they only knew!" Lines are long, airport hallways are dirty, luggage areas are jammed, and airline food gets a little boring. In short, you really don't look forward to your next venture away from home.

Through careful planning, you can make the days you spend away as productive as any day at the office. Consider the trade-offs: What do you have to lose if you work while traveling and what do you have to gain? You probably have very little to lose, because you've tried being a quasi-tourist before. And you have a great deal to gain, because you can accomplish many things away from your hectic office.

One secret to getting something done on a plane trip is to choose your seat carefully. Most domestic flights are now nonsmoking. Most international flights offer travelers a choice between smoking and nonsmoking sections, so both smokers and nonsmokers can be more comfortable. If you are particularly "antismoke," select a seat in the front of the plane—as far away from the smoking section as possible.

Flying first class may be a good strategy for getting a lot of work done. It may be worth the additional cost to have more room, more peace and quiet, and fewer distractions. The flight attendants will be better able to accommodate your needs, as there are fewer passengers to serve. For instance, there's a good chance that they will serve your meal when you want it.

The aisle seat is best for working, especially if you fly coach class. Your writing arm should be on the aisle side for comfort and maneuverability. The disadvantage to the aisle seat, of course, is that you have to get up to let the other passengers in and out.

What kind of work is best done in the air? Reading is an excellent activity. Many travelers enjoy writing reports or answering their correspondence while flying because of the total privacy in the air. Certainly there are hundreds of other people around, but they are not likely to interrupt you. The noise on the plane can easily be shut out. You are left with hours of "quiet time" for handling important projects.

Portable dictating machines make report and letter writing faster and easier than ever for travelers. With these small machines, you can also record various notes to yourself or to your secretary for review later. Once you learn how to use dictating equipment, you will find it far more convenient than writing your thoughts out in longhand.

Many dictating machines on the market are useful in the office, but they do not block out the heavy background noises travelers must contend with in planes and busy airports. How can you tell if you have a good machine? Give your selected model the Douglass Noise Test. Set up your machine on the plane. Wait until the pilot revs the engines, just before takeoff. The flight attendant will begin to announce safety instructions over the public-address system. The level of excitement on the plane will rise as the passengers anticipate takeoff. Now is the time. Speak into your new recorder. If you can hear your dictation on the playback, you have a good machine. If you hear nothing but noise, return the recorder to the store, and get your money back. The machine is no good for traveling. Find a machine that works well under all circumstances.

New electronic technology makes it easier to work on the run. Notebook computers allow you to do almost anything wherever you are. Cellular telephones keep you in touch as you roam. Hand-held scanners, portable printers, and small modems make it possible to be more productive on the move. In some cities there are shops that specialize in turning your car into an electronic office on wheels. The complete electronic office in a briefcase cannot be far behind. When the cellular satellites are in place and functioning, working on trips will be as easy as working in the office. If you travel a lot, you should consider all the electronic devices now available to you. The real trick is to keep up-to-date in this fast-changing field.

Organize Your Briefcase Into a Portable Office

Many of us spend a big part of the workweek traveling from one place to another. Recent studies show that managers spend on average about 10 to 20 percent of their time traveling. Salespeople spend 30 to 40 percent of the week traveling or waiting.

To use travel time for productive work requires preparation. On the road, your briefcase is your traveling desk. You want to be sure it is well organized and ready for action. Arrange your travel briefcase like a mini-office. With everything in its place, you can open the briefcase, get some work done, and close it again at dining or landing time.

Our friend Harold Taylor, a consultant in Canada, has the most organized briefcase we've ever seen. In the larger pockets of his briefcase you will find stationery, file folders, envelopes, scratch pad, reading material, and road maps. In the smaller pockets are a calculator, pens, checkbook, business cards, address book, appointment book, credit cards, and airline schedule book.

However, what makes Harold Taylor unique is what he calls his junk box. It is actually a plastic fishing tackle box that fits neatly in one side of his briefcase. Inside his junk box you will find pens and refills, highlighter pens, Magic Markers, paper clips, stapler and extra staples, rubber bands, U.S. and Canadian coins, penknife, razor-blade cutter, nail clippers, tape measure, glue stick, electronic timer, scissors, screwdriver for eyeglasses, mailing labels, U.S. and Canadian postage stamps, Band-Aids, spare car keys and house keys, batteries and tapes for his dictating machine, needle and thread.

Harold says, "The more organized you become, the less effort it takes to become even more organized." A well-organized briefcase, complete with a junk box—now that is something to think about. No wonder he can get so much work done while traveling.

At the Hotel

You can perform the same types of work activities in the hotel as those you perform on the plane. Indeed, a hotel room offers you a wider choice because you can spread out your materials. Again, the important factor here is preparing ahead of time. Anticipate what you will accomplish during your stay, taking into consideration the appointments and other obligations of your trip. Here are a few guidelines to keep in mind.

1. *Pace your activities.* Consider a variety of things to do. If you can complete an A-1 project or at least make headway on it, you will feel a gratifying sense of accomplishment. But remember to break up your pace. Do other forms of work, background reading, or pleasure reading. Take walks or naps. The demands of travel can be heavy, particularly if you are making time-zone changes. You might also take advantage of the hotel's exercise facilities. The swimming pool or sauna can offer an excellent change of pace after a hard day at work.

2. *Plan your diversions with care.* Resist pressures to engage in nighttime activities if you really aren't interested. Work or rest instead. Don't feel obliged to participate. If there is a purpose in the after-hours get-together, by all means, attend. Carefully consider the purpose of any activity, and act accordingly.

3. *Resist the temptation to eat excessively during your stay.* The abundant food on many business trips can make you sluggish and tired. After some unfortunate stomach reactions and a few too many "good times," many of us have become wiser travelers. We eat less and eat more bland foods while traveling. This helps make our trips more enjoyable.

4. *Do not overdrink.* Time-conscious travelers should also consider the effects of alcohol. An amazing amount of alcohol can be consumed during a business trip. There are drinks at the airport, more drinks on the plane (before and after dinner), a drink following your arrival, a few more in the evening, and of course a nightcap. You need an iron constitution to handle all this; most people can't take it. If they don't wind up absolutely drunk, they will at least be seriously debilitated—at a time when they may be called upon to make important decisions or perform at their peak.

5. *Limit sight-seeing.* You should also consider the pros and cons of extensive sight-seeing during your trip. If you will be staying in a city, you may find some tourist attractions to your liking. Remember, though, that you pay a price if you try to do it all at once. Instead of trying to squeeze in all the sights while you conduct your business,

investigate the special, though lesser-known, attractions of the city. Plan a return visit for your next vacation, and then do the town.

Returning Home

Whether you are a frequent traveler or an infrequent traveler, there are a few activities you should always do on the trip home. While experiences are still fresh in your mind, write any follow-up letters or reports generated by your trip. A quiet plane trip is by far the best time to take care of these concerns. There will generally be new developments once you return to your office that will demand your instant attention. Complete your expense report for costs incurred during the trip. Have it ready for your secretary the moment you walk in the door so you won't have to bother with it later.

Try to complete any paperwork generated on the trip before you get back. You won't have to worry about finding time to finish it when you get back to your office. Call the office. Modem the paperwork. Fax it. Your goal is to have the trip "over" as much as possible when you return. Leftover reports from a trip are difficult and boring once you return and get into other things.

Many people experience an emotional letdown when they return from a trip. This seems to be a problem for both the frequent and the occasional traveler. Even people who have excellent work habits in and out of the office find the transition period difficult. It is hard to psych yourself up for returning to the office routine. People do adjust but not that quickly, and the length of your absence from the office has a direct effect on how long it takes you to readjust. Trips that cross more than three time zones may require special recuperation efforts.

Depending on your body cycle, attitudes, and preferences, you can try one of the two approaches described below to get back into the swing of things. The first approach involves an earlier starting time, and the second, oddly enough, involves a later starting time.

If travel letdown has you dragging, try an earlier starting time to move yourself back into the office routine. "Attack" the next day with a running start. Don't wait until you get to the office to begin work; start at home. Get up fifteen minutes earlier than normal, and do some wake-up exercises. Take a cold shower, and sing a line or two of your favorite tune. After a good breakfast, make a phone call before you head for your car and the office. Open that report you've been dreading and promise yourself you'll draft an outline before you finish your cup of coffee. Whoops! You've begun work without realizing it!

Arrive at the office a few minutes earlier than normal. Those extra minutes could be just what you need to be ready for action when your coworkers arrive. Some people find it useful to set appointments early on their first day back. These morning appointments force them to get it together faster.

Whatever you do, set significant objectives for early in the day. Don't chat about your trip, read the newspaper, or sort through that stack of mail. If you accomplish an important objective during the first hour back at your desk, you will find your travel letdown turning into energetic momentum.

If the above scenario sends you reeling, try the reverse approach—a later starting time. If you've used your travel time well, you needn't feel guilty. Ease back into your routine. If possible, take the morning off to gather your wits. Play a round of golf, watch Oprah Winfrey, or do a little unhurried shopping. Many travelers find suitcases, airports, and taxis both physically and mentally exhausting. You may need a little more recovery time to be at your best.

The more you travel, the more you should view airports, planes, and taxis as an extension of your office. When you master this attitude, you will no longer feel that you've been away from the routine, and reentry will be less of a problem. As you settle into your trip, learn to open your briefcase, shut out extraneous noises, and concentrate on the project at hand. You may find yourself looking forward to uninterrupted travel time so you can get something accomplished.

Travel need not ruin your time-management discipline. If travel is a part of your job, treat it as such, and apply the same time-management principles to your trips as those you use at home. Once you honestly decide that you can control your travel time, you will find many new opportunities to use it better. Learn to make travel time work for you instead of against you.

Scoring Guide for Chapter Nine Quiz

	SA	MA	U	MD	SD
1.	1	2	3	4	5
2.	5	4	3	2	1
3.	1	2	3	4	5
4.	5	4	3	2	1

Ten
Conquering Procrastination

After all is said and done, more is usually said than done.

Old Proverb

Before reading this chapter, please circle your response to each of the following statements. A scoring guide is at the end of the chapter.

SA = Strongly Agree   **MA** = Mildly Agree   **U** = Undecided
MD = Mildly Disagree   **SD** = Strongly Disagree

							Score
1. I often put off tasks that are unpleasant for me.	SA	MA	U	MD	SD		_____
2. I tend to wait until the last minute to get started on things.	SA	MA	U	MD	SD		_____
3. I often have to wait for the right mood, or the right time, to tackle creative work.	SA	MA	U	MD	SD		_____
4. I often worry about making the wrong decision.	SA	MA	U	MD	SD		_____
						Total Score	_____

Procrastination plagues all of us. More plans go astray, more dreams go unfulfilled, and more time is wasted by procrastination than by any other single factor. Procrastination is a major stumbling block for almost everyone seeking to improve his or her use of time. For most of us, procrastination becomes an insidious habit that can ruin our careers, destroy our happiness, and even shorten our lives.

Procrastinating means doing low-priority activities rather than high-priority ones. It is all a matter of priorities. Avery Schreiber the comedian once conducted a seminar with us. We can't remember all the words of a humorous song he sang, but we do remember the chorus:

> *Priorities, think of what you're doin'*
> *Priorities, you may soon be bluin'*
> *Priorities, you'll drive yourself to ruin*
> *If you pick the wrong priorities.*

Procrastinating means straightening your desk when you should be working on that report, calling on the friendly customer who buys very little when you should be preparing a sales presentation for that tough prospect who would buy much more, or watching TV when you should be exercising. Procrastinating means avoiding coworkers rather than telling them bad news or staying away from the office so you do not have to discipline a subordinate. It means postponing activities with your children because you have more urgent things to do at work—only to discover one day that the children are grown and that it is too late to do all the things you talked about doing together.

Procrastination prevents success. Success comes from doing the really important things that lead to results. Yet these important things are usually the very focus of our procrastination. We seldom put off unimportant things. If we could only learn to shift our procrastination from important things to unimportant things, our problem would disappear. One reason we postpone important things is that we tend to confuse them with merely urgent things. We constantly respond to the urgent. Our days are filled with demands and pressures from all quarters. Important things seldom exert this kind of pressure until they reach the crisis state. By responding to the urgent and postponing the important, we guarantee a continual number of crises in our lives.

Tracing the Major Causes of Procrastination

To conquer procrastination, we must understand that it is a habit. Much of what we do, the way we approach things, even the way we think, is based on habit. For most of us, one day looks very much like another. Our lives are full of routines and patterns. To overcome procrastination we undoubtedly have to change our habits, because procrastination breeds procrastination.

From physics we learn that a body at rest tends to remain at rest. Anyone who has ever sat down in an easy chair in front of the TV knows how true this is. It takes greater force to start movement than to sustain movement. To conquer procrastination, we must overcome our inertia—our tendency to resist taking action. Once action is begun, it is more likely to continue. It is the beginning that is difficult. Most of the techniques discussed in this chapter are designed to help you take that first step.

Procrastination can be traced to three major causes. We tend to put off things that are unpleasant, things that are difficult, and things that involve tough decisions. Yet these are the very things that contribute most to our success.

A variety of techniques can be used to conquer procrastination. Not all these techniques will apply to your situation. Some techniques may be personally more appealing than others. To make good use of the concepts presented here, you will need to find the best combination of techniques for your purposes. If a technique works, you are on your way. If it doesn't, try another technique or a different combination of techniques until you find the ones that work best for you.

Unpleasant Tasks

Let's first tackle procrastination caused by unpleasant tasks—for most people, the greatest single cause. When you postpone an unpleasant task, you are attempting to make life easier for yourself by avoiding the distasteful. Ironically, though, putting off the task only increases the unpleasantness, since distasteful tasks seldom disappear.

Often, the best way to handle unpleasant tasks is to do them first. Take a lesson from the little boy who eats his spinach first to get it out of the way so he can enjoy the rest of the meal. Try scheduling your most unpleasant tasks, the ones you tend to put off most often, for the beginning of your day. Get them behind you rather than dread them and continually put them off.

Postponing the unpleasant can be costly, since the work may expand with delay. If you wait until the last possible minute, you will have to work under increased pressure. The longer you wait, the greater the number of things that can go wrong. You've put off that report until the last minute, and suddenly the computer system goes down. You have another crisis on your hands. And the crisis may spread to others. Tempers flare, unkind words are exchanged. Anxiety increases. You become depressed and frustrated with the whole thing. No one works well under these conditions. The quality of your actions is bound to suffer. You dislike yourself, and the pain of the procrastinated report lasts long beyond the crisis itself.

Other costs of delay are not as immediate, but they can be far more serious. For example:

- Delay answering an inquiry and you may lose a customer.
- Delay servicing a machine and you may have a costly break-down.
- Delay developing new products and your competitors will have them first.
- Delay improving your operations and you may lose your competitive advantage.
- Delay exercising and you may shorten your life.
- Delay making a will and your heirs may struggle with red tape and arbitrary court decisions.

Considering the costs of delay may help you get moving. When you are tempted to procrastinate, stop and think for a moment. What problems are you likely to create for yourself? If you don't want to live with those problems, don't procrastinate. Analyze your unpleasant task. Exactly what is it that makes the task unpleasant? Learn to confront the unpleasantness and deal with it directly. Many people challenge themselves to do at least one thing they dread every month. If you do this, you will add a new dimension to your life. You will gain new confidence and respect for yourself as you begin to master some of your fears. The following guidelines can help you get started.

1. *Fragment the work.* Sometimes it helps to tackle unpleasant tasks in small pieces. You can endure anything for a few minutes at a time. Try tackling an unpleasant task for five or ten minutes. You may find that it is not so unpleasant after all once you get moving. And even if you stop after a few minutes, you are still gaining on the total task. For example, you've been planning to start that new exercise program your doctor says you need, but the thought of all that work is too much. Don't focus on an hour at a time. Begin with five minutes.

2. *Set a deadline.* Setting a deadline for the task helps some people get started. The pressure of a deadline, even a self-imposed one, can be sufficient to create action. Make sure your deadline is realistic and put it in writing. Post the written deadline on the wall, set it on your desk, or put it wherever you will see it frequently.

3. *Make your deadline known.* To strengthen your resolve, let other people know about your deadline. We frequently break commitments we make to ourselves, but we are not so likely to break a commitment we make to others. It is painful and embarrassing to admit we haven't

done it. So make a commitment to your spouse, or coworker, or boss, or friend, or whomever you like. Schedule appointments with others to discuss results, set deadlines, and promise action. The risk of losing face will likely spur you to action.

4. *Promise yourself a reward.* Another way to get yourself started and keep going is to promise yourself a reward for completing the task. You might reward yourself with a special lunch for finishing that project you've been putting off, a weekend vacation for painting the house, or a Friday afternoon off for finishing all your assignments by noon. A reward can be anything that appeals to you, whether large or small. There are two main points to remember, though: If you don't earn the reward, don't give it to yourself; and if you do earn it, be sure to take it. Occasional rewards can make life more interesting and at the same time can help you conquer your procrastination.

5. *Delegate unpleasant tasks.* Delegation may be a good way to handle unpleasant tasks. Unfortunately, most people feel guilty about delegating something they don't enjoy doing. If you only delegated junk jobs, such guilt may be appropriate. However, just because you don't enjoy the task, doesn't mean someone else will also find it distasteful. They may actually enjoy tasks that you think are unpleasant. Forget your guilt, and try delegating.

6. *Hire specialized help.* Buying a reprieve is another way to get unpleasant tasks done much faster. For instance, you won't have to continue dreading the thought of painting the living room if you hire a painter to do it. Often the cost of hiring someone makes good sense economically as well as psychologically. How many of your unpleasant tasks could be done by someone else?

Difficult Tasks

Procrastination caused by difficult tasks usually calls for a different approach. Quite often we avoid difficult tasks because we simply don't know where to start. The task may be so complex that it overwhelms us. We need to find some way to reduce the apparent complexity so the task no longer appears difficult.

Quite often it's the difficult, perplexing tasks that give us some of our greatest opportunities. Paul Tournier, in *The Adventure of Living* (New York: Harper & Row, 1965), describes them in terms of adventures:

> There is an astonishing contrast between the heavy perplexity that inhibits before the adventure has begun and the excitement that grips us the moment it begins. . . . As

soon as a man makes up his mind to take the plunge into
adventure, he is aware of a new strength he did not think
he had, which rescues him from all his perplexities.

The following ideas may help you begin your adventure.

1. *Break the job down.* One excellent way to get started is to break
the task down into smaller parts. Keep breaking down the parts until
you can see the first step. Essentially this is a matter of working back-
ward. You start with the desired result, then keep asking yourself
what you have to do to achieve it. Once you have broken the task
down, focus on only one part at a time.

For example, you've been putting off doing a feasibility study for
a new process. Since no one has ever applied this process in your
industry, there are no guidelines to follow. How do you break it down
to smaller parts? Start by outlining the finished report. What should
the key topic be? Then look at each topic and determine what you
need to discuss. What steps must you take to obtain the information
you need? Whom should you talk with? Continue in this fashion until
you've broken the task down into a number of subunits. The subunits
never look as difficult as the entire task.

2. *Find all the minijobs in your project.* Another approach is to break
a task down into "minijobs" that can be accomplished in less than ten
minutes. Assume that you need to prepare a forecast of sales for next
year. You estimate that it will take you thirty hours to complete the
project. Not only is the task difficult, you have no idea where you will
find the hours you need. So you keep putting it off. How can you
break the project down into minijobs? Within a few minutes, you
might be able to get a copy of last year's forecast, locate the file you
will need, determine what information will be required, decide whom
you must contact, arrange appointments with other people, request
additional information, or assign parts of the project to others. As you
begin to think about it, you will come up with many minijobs that
can be done in less than ten minutes.

An added benefit to this approach is that you can do the minijobs
during odd moments of the day that would otherwise be wasted. At
the same time, performing the tasks will lead you to your goal. To
make the approach work best, prepare a list of all the short tasks you
will need to do to complete the project. Then you won't have to think
them up again each time you find a few odd moments. Establish priorities so you can start on the most important tasks first. After you
have finished several of the short tasks, you may discover that the
project is not as overwhelming or as difficult as you thought. You may

come up with a few shortcuts. You may find it easier to schedule large blocks of time to finish it. The main point is that the short tasks will get you started. The more you get done, the easier it is to keep going.

3. *Find a leading task.* Another technique to help you get started is to find a leading task. Again, consider that report you've been putting off. One obvious way to begin is to make notes on the points you need to cover. If even this seems too much to tackle, try sharpening your pencil. A leading task should be extremely easy and quick and should not require planning. It should entail very little conscious effort on your part. Rolling a sheet of paper into the typewriter can lead to typing that letter. Picking up the telephone can lead to calling on new customers. Buying a paintbrush can lead to resuming your art lessons. You certainly can't finish until you start.

4. *Be creative.* Sometimes the difficult task you keep postponing calls for creative thought. You keep saying that you're waiting for inspiration or for the right moment to strike. Someone once said that inspiration is 90 percent perspiration. If you wait for inspiration, it seldom appears. A little physical action is what you need. One author we know waited three years for the inspiration to begin writing his book. A friend finally convinced him to set aside thirty minutes each day for writing. He could write whatever he wanted, as long as he wrote for the entire thirty minutes. For the first two weeks the author wrote nonsense phrases, paragraphs about the weather, poetry, notes to himself, and other nonproductive pieces. Gradually, though, his writing began to become more serious. He began outlining ideas for his novel—short descriptions of characters, various ideas for plots. Before long, he was writing his novel. Don't wait for inspiration. Take action now.

5. *Make your moods work for you.* "I'm not in the mood" is another common excuse for putting things off. The trick is to take advantage of your moods rather than have your moods take advantage of you. Occasionally, it may be best to wait until your mood is right before starting a task. However, there is usually some aspect of the task that will fit your current mood. You may not feel like papering the kitchen today, but you might at least be willing to select the wallpaper. When you find yourself procrastinating because your mood is wrong, ask yourself, "Is there anything, no matter how small, that I am willing to do?" Once you find something you're willing to do—and do it—you're on the way to making your moods work for instead of against you.

6. *Give yourself a pep talk.* Often when you say you're not in the right mood you're busy feeling sorry for yourself. A general lack of motivation or feeling of depression has set in. What you need is a pep

talk. Find a corner to stand in and talk to yourself—out loud. Really lay it on the line! Build yourself up. You can't do anything until you believe you can. A little positive thinking may be what you need. A pep talk is one good way to get yourself going in the right direction again.

7. *Get more information.* Things often seem difficult because we don't know enough about them. Lack of familiarity can lead to lack of interest. The more you know about something, the more you want to know and the more likely you are to get involved and excited. So read a book, attend a lecture, talk with people who know. A short course in auto mechanics may prompt you to make those needed repairs on your automobile. Finding a photo of your great-grandmother may get you started on developing your family tree. Learning about linear programming may make you excited about solving the inventory-control problem in your office.

Indecision

Indecision is the third major cause of procrastination. It usually stems from a strong desire to be right, a strong desire to avoid being wrong, or a desire for perfection.

There is a time to deliberate and a time to act. The time to decide is when further information will add very little to the quality of the decision. Delay beyond that point seldom helps. No one is right all the time. Often there simply is no right or wrong involved. Make a sincere effort to obtain the best information possible within the time you have available. Then make the decision and move on. Above all, don't keep fretting and fussing over the decision, and don't keep re-hashing it.

Perfectionism is often the cause of indecision. Budding authors who keep rewriting the first chapter, striving for the perfect phrase, seldom publish books. Managers who keep pushing their subordinates for perfect results seldom achieve them.

Perfectionism strikes about 40 percent of us, some to a greater degree than others. At least 20 percent of us are real fuss-budgets. We expect too much of ourselves, and we also place impossible demands on others.

Perfectionists tend to set goals they simply can't meet, yet, since they measure their self-worth by their achievements, they suffer from low self-esteem. As a result, perfectionists experience more anxiety and depression. Perfectionists also make life miserable for those around them, straining relationships and accomplishing little. Failing terrifies them, yet, in an ironic twist of fate, perfectionists with high standards are more likely to fail. They are often less productive and don't earn any more money than their nonperfectionistic colleagues.

Perfectionists often major in minors; they get so involved with trivia that they completely miss the larger issues. Perfectionists have a hard time setting priorities because everything seems to be equally important. There are no degrees of perfection. They spend far too much time, effort, and money on a job. Ironically, they often miss the deadlines, too. Their jobs, and their lives, become oppressive, and they suffer from burnout more than nonperfectionists.

However, you can reduce perfectionistic tendencies. First, list the advantages and disadvantages of trying to be perfect. Second, strive for "good" performance instead of "best" performance. The key is to do things well enough to produce the desired results, and then stop. Don't continue beyond that point, seeking perfection.

Perfectionists might benefit by trying to relax and to loosen up. A Chinese proverb says, "Life is too important to be taken seriously." Learn to laugh, especially at yourself and your foibles. Change the way you talk to yourself. Stop reciting all the "shoulds" that occur to you. Most of them are only self-imposed, artificial standards. Allow yourself to enjoy life like your "imperfect" friends.

Becoming less perfect may be difficult, and it may take awhile, but it is worth the effort. You will live longer, you will live better, others will like you more.

Indecisiveness can also be traced to vague worries and fears that something will go wrong. We all encounter obstacles at one time or another. But you should not borrow trouble or procrastinate because of vague worries. Instead, focus on what you want to accomplish. Write down all the obstacles or problems that might prevent you from achieving your goal. Review the problems and think of various ways you might solve them. Write down all the possible solutions and pick the ones most likely to work for you. You now have a basis for positive planning that will take you beyond your procrastination.

Another way to overcome your vague worries and fears is to develop a worry list. Write down all the things you worry about, all the things you think might go wrong, all the horrible things you think might happen. From time to time, read over the list and note what has actually happened. You will probably find that most of the things you worry about never happen. A worry list can help you worry less.

Taking Preventive Action

Changing your do-it-later urge into a do-it-now habit requires positive action. Things don't just happen. Things happen because people make them happen. Do things differently. Answer your mail as soon as you open it. Don't set it aside for later. Whenever you say to yourself, "I've got to do something about that," do something about it now, not later. Schedule things and live by your schedule. Learn to check those impulses to do unscheduled things—impulses that often hide your procrastination. Learn to do the most important things first.

Procrastination is a psychological problem, and a victory over procrastination is essentially a psychological victory. You may have to play games with yourself in order to overcome your inertia and change the habits that hamper your progress. However, as an old proverb states, "The more you do of what you're doing, the more you'll get of what you're getting." If you want different results, you must change your approach.

Take some time to analyze your procrastination habits. Begin by answering the following questions:

1. What things do I tend to put off most often?
2. What things am I currently putting off?
3. How do I know when I'm procrastinating? Do I have a set of favorite replacement activities?
4. How do I feel about my procrastination?
5. What happens when I procrastinate? Are the results positive or negative?
6. What causes my procrastination? (Try to link a specific cause to each procrastinated task.)
7. What can I do to overcome procrastination? (List specific steps you can take to get started and set deadlines on them.)

The easiest way to overcome procrastination is to never let it happen in the first place. There are two things you can do. First, clarify your objectives. Setting objectives is the best way to cope with daily problems and pressures. Make sure you are pursuing the right things for you. Often what you think you want to do is not what you really want to do. So you put things off. Your procrastination is a subconscious message that your priorities are out of focus. If you continually think through your objectives and priorities and focus your efforts on what's most important, you will seldom be bothered by procrastination.

Second, develop the habit of planning every day. Ask yourself what you want to accomplish with each day. Write out a list of things to do and then follow your plan. Do the most important things first. If you develop the habit of making a list of things to do each day, and then do them, you will find that procrastination is something that happens only to other people.

Procrastination is a habit—a very bad habit. The more you procrastinate, the more likely you are to continue to procrastinate in the future. The more you resist the temptation to put things off, the easier it is to continue resisting. Do everything you can to develop a do-it-now habit.

The most valuable thing you can do when you are procrastinating is to admit it. As long as you continue to deny or rationalize your procrastination you are not in a position to overcome it. Once you admit that you are indeed procrastinating, examine your situation and determine why. Then find a technique for conquering your procrastination. In the end procrastination, like any problem, can be solved only by positive action. Remember, there are only two rules for accomplishing anything: Rule 1: Get started. Rule 2: Keep going.

Scoring Guide for Chapter Ten Quiz					
	SA	**MA**	**U**	**MD**	**SD**
1.	1	2	3	4	5
2.	1	2	3	4	5
3.	1	2	3	4	5
4.	1	2	3	4	5

Eleven
Managing Stress and Change

Rule No. 1: Don't sweat the small stuff.
Rule No. 2: It's all small stuff.

> Robert Eliot, M.D.
> *Is It Worth Dying For?*

Before reading this chapter, please circle your response to each of the following statements. A scoring guide is at the end of the chapter.

sa = Strongly Agree   MA = Mildly Agree   U = Undecided
MD = Mildly Disagree   SD = Strongly Disagree

		Score
1. I laugh a lot, and have a really good time, both at work and at home.	SA MA U MD SD	_____
2. People often tell me I should slow down or relax.	SA MA U MD SD	_____
3. I usually get plenty of sleep, exercise regularly, and eat healthy foods.	SA MA U MD SD	_____
4. I feel a lot of stress, tension, and pressure at work, and I have trouble handling it well.	SA MA U MD SD	_____
	Total Score	_____

Stress can be a major factor affecting the way we use our time. Most of us fear stress. We don't understand it. We try to escape or avoid it. But stress is unavoidable, and a certain amount of stress is even necessary for good performance. The trick, of course, is to maintain the proper balance.

Stress is defined as any action or situation that places special physical or psychological demands. Anything abnormal can throw us into a state of disequilibrium, and we react by attempting to bring the body back into equilibrium. It is this reaction that creates most of the stress symptoms we know so well. Since stress is associated with disequilibrium, it is also frequently associated with change. Change creates new situations. With new situations, we must establish new patterns of living that will bring us back to a state of equilibrium. Positive change can have just as much stressful impact as negative change.

Most of us think of stress as something to be avoided, but some stress is necessary to perform effectively. Too little stress can be harmful. Figure 11-1 shows the relationship between stress and performance. Note that as stress increases, so does performance—up to a point. Beyond that point, stress hampers performance. The idea is to have just enough—but not too much.

The curve on Figure 11-1 explains why many of us seem to do better under the pressure of a close deadline. The approaching deadline creates a stress reaction that stimulates performance. However, if we are already close to the top of the curve, the stress from the approaching deadline could be enough to put us over the top, causing a decrease in performance.

How much stress is too much? This varies from person to person. In terms of stress, researchers have discovered that there are basically

Figure 11-1. Stress and performance curve.

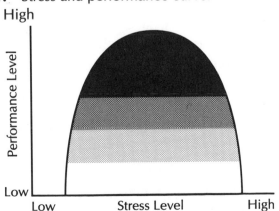

two types of people: racehorses and turtles. Racehorses thrive on high stress levels. They are happy with vigorous, fast-paced life-styles. Turtles are happier in peaceful, quiet environments. Either type, if placed in the opposite environment, will function poorly. A big danger, of course, lies in mistaking your type. If you incorrectly believe you are a racehorse, you will push beyond your normal stress endurance. If you wrongly believe you are a turtle, you will live a life of frustration.

Analyzing the Effects of Stress

Stress affects people in three ways: emotionally, behaviorally, and physiologically. The emotional changes are the ones many people commonly associate with stress. These range from feelings of mild annoyance to blustering rage; from slight anxiety to overpowering fear; from amusement to ecstasy. The behavioral changes brought on by stress can be positive or negative: Moderate stress may bring about improvements in performance; severe stress can lead to greater errors and even to accidents.

The physiological changes created by stress are the most significant, for they concern matters of life and death. Stress can lead to a wide variety of physical ailments and life-threatening diseases, including peptic ulcers, migraines, hypertension, rheumatoid arthritis, backaches, emphysema, ulcerative colitis, asthma, mental disease, cancer, and heart attack.

The body's automatic reaction to stress is often called the "fight or flight" response: The body prepares for either action by releasing hormones into the bloodstream that activate the autonomic nervous system. Since the autonomic nervous system controls involuntary body muscles, such as those that alter blood pressure and digestion, the body undergoes many changes. Hearing and smelling become more acute. Pupils dilate to admit extra light. Breathing is deeper and faster. Mucous membranes in the nose and throat shrink to make wider passages for the increased air flow. The heart pumps extra blood, sending more food and oxygen to the brain, lungs, and muscles for greater strength and energy. Blood clots more quickly, helping to prevent loss of blood in case of injury. Increased perspiration flushes wastes and cools the overactive body system. The body conserves its energy for top-priority functions by shutting down lower-priority activities.

These physiological reactions to stress prepare the body to fight or flee. When either route is taken, the system naturally restores itself. The problem today is that very few of the situations that create stress allow for either action. Most stress situations are psychological rather than physical. This is one of the penalties of modern civilization.

Analyzing the Symptoms of Stress

Each of us responds to stress with a particular set of symptoms. Our specific response is determined by our genetic heritage, our training, our outlook on life, and other variables. Whatever our response to stress, we should keep in mind that dysfunctional stress symptoms signal a breakdown in the most vulnerable parts of the body. Dr. Hans Selye, the noted expert on stress, identified the common signs of dysfunctional stress—or what Dr. Selye termed "distress." These include:

- General irritability
- Increased heart rate
- Dryness of throat or mouth
- Impulsive behavior
- Emotional instability
- Tendency to vacillate in making decisions
- Inability to concentrate
- Accident proneness
- Tendency to overemphasize trifles
- Tendency to midjudge people
- Feelings of persecution
- Forgetfulness
- Decrease in sex drive
- Fatigue
- Vague feelings of dissatisfaction
- Insomnia
- Excessive sweating
- Frequent need to urinate
- Migraine headaches
- Loss of appetite
- Excessive eating
- Missed menstrual cycles
- Premenstrual tension
- Pain in lower back or neck
- Trembling or nervous tics
- Increased smoking

- Increased use of alcohol
- Increased use of prescribed drugs such as tranquilizers
- Procrastination
- Inability to get organized
- Confusion about duties
- Uncertainty about whom to trust
- Stuttering and other speech difficulties

Learn to be a good judge of your own stress symptoms. You don't need a complex scientific test. You can develop an instinctive feel for when you're running at too high or too low a stress level. When you know you've had enough, it's time to quit.

Measure Your Stress

Because the body neither fights nor runs, stress reactions tend to accummulate and become prolonged. This is when ailments and disease enter the picture. Under chronic stress, people are ripe for an organic crisis. Thomas Holmes and Richard Rahe, psychiatrists at the University of Washington Medical School, have done pioneering work relating stress to disease. They developed a yardstick for evaluating personal stress called the Life Events Scale (or Social Readjustment Rating Scale). Look at the scale in Figure 11-2 to evaluate your potential stress problems.

According to Holmes and Rahe, some life events create more stress than others. A life crisis is defined as the accumulation of at least 150 points in a twelve-month period. The body is "at risk" for the twenty-four months following a life crisis. The risk factors for moderate, medium, and severe life crises are shown in Figure 11-3. More points mean a greater chance of illness and a greater chance that the illness will be serious.

The Holmes-Rahe theory linking stress and disease is not perfect, but it is certainly cause for reflection. The accumulation of 300 or more points in a single year indicates an almost 80 percent chance of a health change! Furthermore, the greater the points, the more serious the health change. Given this fact, it would seem advisable to stretch significant changes over long periods to reduce the danger of facing a life crisis. As Alvin Toffler pointed out in *Future Shock* (New York: Random House, 1970), the rate of change can be even more devastating than the change itself. This is particularly significant when we realize that many of the changes taking place around us are beyond our control.

Figure 11-2. The social readjustment rating scale.

Life Event	Points
1. Death of spouse	100
2. Divorce	73
3. Marital separation	65
4. Jail term	63
5. Death of close family member	63
6. Personal injury or illness	53
7. Marriage	50
8. Fired at work	47
9. Marital reconciliation	45
10. Retirement	45
11. Change in health of family member	44
12. Pregnancy	40
13. Sex difficulties	39
14. Gain of new family member	39
15. Business readjustment	39
16. Change in financial state	38
17. Death of close friend	37
18. Change to different line of work	36
19. Change in number of arguments with spouse	35
20. Mortgage over $10,000	31
21. Foreclosure of mortgage or loan	30
22. Change in responsibilities at work	29
23. Son or daughter leaving home	29
24. Trouble with in-laws	29
25. Outstanding personal achievement	28
26. Wife begins or stops work	26
27. Begin or end school	26
28. Change in living conditions	25
29. Revision of personal habits	24
30. Trouble with boss	23
31. Change in work hours or work conditions	20
32. Change in residence	20
33. Change in schools	20
34. Change in recreation	19
35. Change in church activities	19
36. Change in social activities	18
37. Mortgage or loan of less than $10,000	17
38. Change in sleeping habits	16
39. Change in number of family get-togethers	15

(continued)

Figure 11-2.   continued.

Life Event	Points
40. Change in eating habits	15
41. Vacation	13
42. Christmas	12
43. Minor violation of the law	11

Source: T. H. Holmes and R. H. Rahe, "The Social Readjustment Rating Scale," *Journal of Psychosomatic Research* (November 1967): 213–218.

Alleviating Stress Symptoms

If stress is unavoidable, what can you do to decrease it? There are several ways to alleviate the problem. None of these techniques will prevent or eliminate stress, but they can dissipate the stress reaction and help you function better.

1. *Get adequate rest.* When you're tired, you're in even worse shape to cope with stress. And since high stress often results in insomnia, you may find it harder than ever to get the proper sleep.

Normal adults need between six and a half and nine hours of sleep every night. Sleep research shows that some of us sleep too much, others sleep too little, and still others vacillate back and forth between too little and too much. Few of us get the right amount regularly. Ironically, the symptoms of too much sleep are almost exactly the same as the ones for too little sleep.

Adequate sleep means getting your necessary minimum every night. It doesn't mean getting too little during the week and then trying to catch up on the weekend. Doing it that way means you are out of phase all the time.

Researchers point out that an increasing number of us are not getting enough sleep. An extra hour of sleep at night might be the best thing you could do. Experiment to discover your minimum need for sleep. You may even want to visit a sleep lab to have your sleep needs tested.

2. *Follow a healthy diet.* Stress can deplete your body's store of certain vitamins. When his happens, your body is less able to counter infections and to function well. Under stress, many people change their eating habits for the worse. They often drink more alcohol too, which complicates the problem. Adequate nutrition is especially important when you're under stress.

Thousands of books have been written about diets. Some make

Figure 11-3. Stress risk factors.

Points Accumulated Over Past Twelve Months:	Probability of Health Change
Moderate (150–199 points)	.37
Medium (200–299 points)	.51
Severe (300 or more points)	.79

sense while others are sometimes ridiculous. Diet is simply control over the kind of fuel you provide your body, and good fuel allows for better performance.

While we do not advocate one diet over another, we do know that most nutritional experts agree that the best diet is one with a minimum of sugar, salt, fat, cholesterol, caffeine, and alcohol. This strikes too close to home for many of us, especially around a holiday season. However, the experts are right. Test it for yourself, especially with sugar. The less sugar you eat, the more energy you have. It's incredible.

The California Board of Health has been campaigning to improve eating habits and now recommends eating five half-cup servings of fresh fruits and vegetables every day. Most of us don't even get close to that standard. However, if we did, we would also be getting closer to what the nutritional experts advise. It is clear that we need more fruits, vegetables, grains, and fiber in our diets—and a lot less junk. If you are concerned about your diet, you also might consider taking vitamins or other nutritional supplements.

Exactly what do you eat—how much and how often? Keep a detailed record of your food intake for a few weeks. The results may surprise you. Not only will a good diet help you cope with stress better; it will give you more energy. High-energy people almost always manage their time better than low-energy people.

3. *Exercise regularly.* Regular, aerobic exercise is excellent for dissipating stress. Before you embark on strenuous activity, consult your physician for advice on a program suited to your needs and abilities. Pick an exercise you enjoy, and make it part of your regular schedule.

Perhaps you are already part of the growing number of people who are exercising more. Then, again, maybe you aren't. We all know the value of exercising, even if we aren't doing much. In fact, the main difference between not exercising thirty years ago and not exercising today is that today you will feel more guilty about it.

Dr. Kenneth Cooper, the late high priest of exercise, said that you should exercise three or four times weekly. You need to get your heart rate up to about 75 percent of its maximum capacity for at least eighteen minutes. With warm-up and cool-down periods, you will need about thirty minutes for your exercise session to be effective.

What kind of exercise you do is less important than doing it regularly. Dr. Cooper suggested many ways to accomplish the same benefit (Kenneth Cooper, *The Aerobics Way*, New York: Bantam Books, 1977), but of the best exercises turns out to be walking. You can do it at any age, anytime, anywhere. A regular walk will probably take inches off your waist and add years to your life.

To boost your energy level during the day, morning exercise is best. Exercise raises the oxygen level of the blood. You are more alert, wide awake, and eager to go. Of course, evening exercise does all this, too, plus it is a great way to unwind and shed the tensions of the day.

Exercise offers a double advantage. In addition to releasing stress, it can help develop the cardiovascular system. Any exercise that demands intense effort for twenty to thirty minutes will probably accomplish both. Jogging, running, tennis, racquetball, basketball, swimming, cycling, squash, and cross-country skiing are excellent. And, as mentioned, even walking can do wonders. Many people who have begun vigorous exercise programs report fewer stress symptoms, increased physical and mental stamina, greater work capacity, and a trimmer body.

4. *Develop positive attitudes.* Did you know that your attitude affects your energy level? Medical research studies show that it only takes 60 percent as much energy to be cheerful as it does to be grumpy. Dr. Norman Vincent Peale, author of *The Power of Positive Thinking* (New York: Prentice-Hall, 1956), has been saying this for many years. However, we now have scientific proof.

A team of doctors studied the effects of attitudes for several years. They actually measured the energy flow during various moods. Their conclusion is powerful: Positive attitudes conserve energy, whereas negative attitudes dissipate it.

Most of us think we are more positive than we actually are. It may be worthwhile to test yourself. For example, what do you think about while you are grooming and dressing in the morning? What are your thoughts while driving to work? What do you think or say if you get caught in a traffic jam? How do you respond to the daily crises, interruptions, and disappointments in your job?

Dr. Peale says that you can divide the world into two groups based on how they get up in the morning. Group one jumps out of bed greeting the day with an exuberant, "Good morning, Lord! I'm ready for an exciting day!" Group two crawls out of bed muttering something like, "Good Lord, it's morning." Which group are you in?

According to Dr. Peale, our attitudes are primarily the result of the words we use when we talk to ourselves. Examined closely, many of us talk in a negative way to ourselves a good part of the time. With some of us, we don't even have to look very close. Our words are very important. Positive words create positive attitudes and conserve energy.

To help you talk in a positive manner, listen to humorous tapes. It is hard to feel gloomy and negative while you are laughing. Whatever it takes, do everything you can to use positive words to yourself all the time. Try to enjoy your work. Forget about harboring grudges. Learn to look at things positively.

5. *Listen to relaxing music.* Music stimulates an emotional response. Try listening to relaxing, soothing music. Let yourself float with the melody. Imagine yourself in a serene environment. Let the music relax your muscles.

We all have our own personal preferences about music. Again, we do not advocate a particular kind of music. Listen to whatever helps you relax. However, there is one type of music you may want to experiment with.

Any music with sixty beats a minute affects us in a special way. Sixty-cycle music has a special quality to it. Research shows that sixty-cycle music automatically increases an alpha brain wave, the relaxation wavelength. Whether or not you like this kind of music is not the point. The effect is automatic. Your body systems will benefit regardless of your personal feelings or opinions.

There is a huge body of literature about this kind of music. An excellent summary is the book *Superlearning* (Sheila Ostrander and Nancy Schroeder with Nancy Ostrander, New York: Dell Publishing, 1979). Libraries can provide reams of material and research studies under the headings of suggestopedia, suggestology, super learning, or accelerated learning.

Most sixty-cycle music is classical. The composers Bach, Corelli, Handel, and Vivaldi composed many works in this range. There is an extensive music list in *Superlearning*. A few current composers are producing this music especially for its relaxation and learning value. Nightingale-Conant Corporation of Chicago (7300 Lehigh Ave., Chicago, IL 60648, Tel. 1-800-323-5552), produces at least two audiocassette albums of sixty-cycle music. Check it out, and test it for yourself.

6. *Try autonomic relaxation exercises.* The value of relaxation exercises designed to trigger the release of the autonomic nervous system

has long been recognized. The exercises consist of tensing particular muscle groups, holding the tense position for several seconds, and then relaxing the muscles. The exercises can be done in about fifteen minutes. Here's how they work. Assume a comfortable body position. Concentrate on tensing and then relaxing different muscle groups one at a time. Start with your toes and progress upward to your legs, trunks, and arms, and finally your head. Eventually, your entire body will feel relaxed. Several cassette tapes are available to guide you through these exercises.

7. *Take a break.* When you feel yourself tensing up, leave the situation. Take a walk around the block. Go shopping. Do anything to break the pattern and give yourself a release.

Vacations are also a good way to provide a break in the pattern. But don't make your vacations as hectic or competitive as your daily routine. You'll only be trading one stress situation for another. If you can't take a long vacation, try several weekend holidays. Do something relaxing.

Do something fun. Too many of us don't seem to have much fun anymore. Plan it, schedule it, make it happen regularly. Remember this cliché: "All work and no play makes Jack a dull boy." Make sure you have the right amount of play time in your life. Time spent in good-hearted pleasure is *not* a waste of time.

8. *Talk it out.* Stress can often be reduced by talking things over with someone else. A listener doesn't even have to respond. He or she can simply serve as a sounding board and help guide your conversation. You can talk things out with a family member, friend, minister, counselor, psychologist, or anyone who is a good listener. Many cities even have organizations that provide professional "listeners" for just this purpose.

9. *Slow down.* Stress often makes people feel rushed, but rushing only increases the pressure. Practice going slower. Eat slowly. Breathe slowly and deeply. Slow your walking pace. Don't speak so rapidly. Repeat what others have said before you respond. You'll understand them better and learn patience as well. Don't try to do everything at once. Don't make too many changes at the same time. String things out a bit. Pace your life better.

10. *Do something for others.* Sometimes stress causes people to focus even more on themselves. This often leads to self-doubt or self-pity. Instead of focusing on yourself, try helping others. In addition to taking your mind off your problems, you will render a valuable contribution and may even make new friends.

The Link Between Stress and Time Management

All time-management concepts are aimed at helping people make sense out of the turmoil of modern life. If you systematically follow the approach to time described in this book, your stress level will decrease. Evaluate your present time use. Identify your top priorities. Plan your days and weeks. Schedule the important activities. Follow your plan. Practicing good time-management techniques can help reduce stress levels while it increases your performance.

If you learn to plan your time carefully, you can feel confident that you are handling the situation to the best of your ability. This knowledge alone can relieve some of the pressure, because you simply can do no more than your time and abilities permit.

Learning to control your environment can go a long way toward reducing stress-generating events. Many of the time wasters that contribute to stress can be eliminated or controlled. This book is devoted to helping you control your time and minimize wasted effort. Remember, though, that not everything can be controlled. Some things are simply beyond your influence. It helps to keep in mind the Serenity Prayer:

> *God, grant me the serenity to accept*
> *the things I cannot change,*
> *The courage to change those*
> *things I can,*
> *And the wisdom to know the difference.*

Mastering Change

Change is the greatest component of stress, yet change is inevitable. It is the new reality. In the words of Al Jolson, "You ain't heard nothin' yet, folks." There are more changes to cope with, and they are happening faster. The faster the change, the greater the stress. Whether positive or negative, change means stress.

William Bridges, in *Making Sense of Life's Changes* (Reading, Mass.: Addison-Wesley, 1980), describes three transition stages created by change: endings, neutral, and new beginnings. In any change, we go through these three stages. When change is positive, we may move through the stages quickly. When the change is negative, it could take weeks, months, or years to get through them.

The *endings* stage is a separation from the past, a discarding of the old ways of behaving. This may be exciting, or it may be a symbolic death. We are thrown off balance and experience a loss. If we see the change as positive, the sense of loss may be brief. If we see the change as negative we may feel the loss for a long time. Pressure to adjust prolongs this stage.

In his book *Helping Employees Cope With Change* (Buffalo, N.Y.: PAT Publications, 1988), George Truell presents a simple model to help explain the endings stage. When change occurs, we experience loss in one or more of four dimensions. He uses the acronym LOSS to describe the four reactions:

1. *Loose ends.* We are confused, temporarily lost, and disoriented. We experience a sense of emptiness, and don't understand what's happening or why. Our energy is spent on "busy work" and on seeking detailed information.

2. *Out of it.* We pull back, withdraw, and disengage from the organization. We wait to see what will happen next, lose interest, and simply "go through the motions." We may avoid people or stay away from work. Our energy is spent insulating ourselves from others.

3. *Sad.* We are depressed. Familiar routines, comfortable relationships, and known support systems are upset. Our identity and way of life are in jeopardy. Our status, or what once had meaning, is now gone. We are no longer certain of who we are, and we feel vulnerable and worry about the future. Our energy is spent talking about the past.

4. *Sour.* We are irritated, upset, and angry. We feel that someone has done something to us, and we don't like it. We feel tricked, deceived, and victimized. Our sense of fairness and justice has been violated, and our anger may be expressed overtly or covertly. Our energy is spent attacking others and seeking revenge.

The neutral stage is a sort of "time-out" phase between the old and the new. It provides time to sort things out, time to explore what has happened and what it all means. During this period, we are both rational and emotional. We need time to sort out our feelings so that our emotions can come into sync with our intellect.

The new beginnings stage is where we begin to experience a sense of reintegration, become involved again, and are fully committed to the change situation. New and different ways of thinking and behaving appear, and we experience a new sense of purpose, renewed interest, and increased energy.

Learn Strategies for Handling Change

Use the following guidelines to help you handle change.

1. *Examine your emotions.* Why are you feeling the way you do? What is it that you are afraid of? What do you really fear losing? Are your fears based on fact or fiction? Learn to accept your fears, analyze them, and act to resolve them.

2. *Realize that your reactions are normal.* Everyone goes through the same process, although some go through it faster than others. It depends on the intensity of the change. Don't feel guilty for reacting to the change. Very few people warmly embrace rapid change.

3. *Be patient with yourself.* You need to forget the past and focus on the present. But don't be in too big a hurry. Don't make rash decisions. Everyone will not adjust at the same rate.

4. *Review your past successes.* Think about all the past changes you have lived through and how well things have turned out. What you did before, you can do again.

5. *Take comfort in those things that have not changed.* Although it may seem like everything has changed, chances are they haven't. Identify what is still the same, and what has actually changed. You will probably find that there are several things that have not changed at all. Things are seldom as black or white as we tend to think they are when our world has been tipped upside down.

6. *Seek support from others.* Offer others your support too. Most of us do not make significant changes in our lives without the support of other people. Look for a support group, or develop one if necessary.

7. *Be confident.* Build up your self-confidence. People with a high sense of confidence handle change much better than those with low self-confidence. Those of us who expect to come out on top are the ones most likely to do so. Challenge yourself to face your fears. Psychologist Eden Ryl advises us to do something we fear every month just because we fear it. Doing this increases our willingness to take risks and boosts our self-confidence.

8. *Be creative.* Use the change as an opportunity to try something new or different. Force yourself out of your comfort zone. Brainstorm for new ideas. Get others to help you brainstorm. Anticipate future changes, and prepare for them. Increase your knowledge to open up more options for yourself.

9. *Be healthy, fit, and positive.* All the suggestions above for handling stress also apply to change. Remember, change is the largest

component of stress. Get plenty of rest, eat healthy, exercise, maintain positive attitudes, laugh a lot.

10. *Don't give up.* An old proverb says, "We cannot direct the wind, but we can adjust the sail." Where there is life, there is hope. Change means adjustment. We may not want to adjust, but we can nonetheless do it. Learning to cope well with stress and change offers countless rewards. The alternative is to risk poor health, poor performance, wasted time, and a wasted life.

	SA	MA	U	MD	SD
Scoring Guide for Chapter Eleven Quiz					
1.	5	4	3	2	1
2.	1	2	3	4	5
3.	5	4	3	2	1
4.	1	2	3	4	5

Twelve
Balancing Your Life

Dost thou love life? Then do not squander time, for that is the stuff life is made of.

Benjamin Franklin
Poor Richard's Almanac

Before reading this chapter, please circle your response to each of the following statements. A scoring guide is at the end of the chapter.

SA = Strongly Agree   MA = Mildly Agree   U = Undecided
MD = Mildly Disagree   SD = Strongly Disagree

Score

1. I have a written list of long-range personal goals.
SA MA U MD SD _____

2. I feel like I don't have enough time for family, leisure, or other personal interests away from work.
SA MA U MD SD _____

3. I feel a lot of satisfaction with my life.
SA MA U MD SD _____

4. I constantly look for things that waste my personal time and try to eliminate or reduce them.
SA MA U MD SD _____

Total Score _____

Hard as it is for some people to believe, there is more to life than work. One of the prime reasons for managing our time is to reduce our workweek and gain more personal time. Time management is a basic consideration in every aspect of our lives. Just as we should be concerned about how to best use our work time, so we should be concerned about how to best use our personal time. Work time is measured in terms of work-related objectives; personal time is measured in terms of satisfaction, emotional gain, quality of relationships, fulfillment, or service to others.

Many of us live our lives as though we were in training for the future. Unlike a game, life has no time-outs, no instant replays, no practice sessions. All time is real time; every day counts. We often postpone living. There are so many things we want to do—someday. Someday is a myth. It never arrives because it was here all the time. To enrich our lives, we must act now. We should ask ourselves this question: "If I were to die today, would I be pleased with the way I have spent my time?" Few of us could truthfully answer yes.

Clarifying Personal Goals

If we can't do anything about the past, we can certainly do something about the future. We can start by clarifying our personal goals. Clarifying goals is more a matter of finding a direction than of defining specific end points. Life is found in the running, not in the arrival. When we know the things that are really important to us, we are amazed at the number of opportunities we have to obtain them. But if we never clarify our objectives, our opportunities remain hidden.

Certainly our time is not entirely our own to do with as we please. Our boss, spouse, children, friends, and others make legitimate demands on our time. Yet most of us resist having our time and our lives defined for us. We seek more autonomy, more freedom to decide how to spend our time.

The paradox of time applies to our personal lives as well as to our work lives: We never have enough time to do everything we'd like to do, yet we have all the time there is. Furthermore, there is always enough time to do what is most important to us—if we only knew what that was.

What do we really want to do? If we cannot answer this question, our lives will be aimless. Even when we realize that we can do almost anything we want, we often settle for spending our time the same way other people spend their time. We will come to believe that whatever it is we really want to do we cannot do because of circumstances, human nature, or the fear of what others might think. Finally, we quit analyzing it and say that there just isn't enough time.

Most of us operate with an intermediate personal time horizon. We think in terms of days, weeks, and occasionally months. We rarely think in terms of minutes, and in fact we never even consider our idle minutes as a waste of time. Nor do we think in terms of years or lifetimes—in terms of how the present is related to the future. So we start over each day. As a result, we lead a random, unfocused existence. We have the vague sense that we are going nowhere, but we don't know why.

What do you wish were happening in your life? What do you wish you had time for? The concepts outlined in this book for solving work time problems also apply to personal time problems. There are personal activity traps, just as there are work activity traps. People become so engrossed in personal activities that they cease to ask themselves about the purpose and value of those activities.

To manage your personal life effectively means asking yourself what kind of life you want to lead, what kind of person you want to be. You can't plan for the present without also planning for the future. Tomorrow is connected to today just as today was connected to yesterday. You cannot afford to leave those connections to chance.

Changing the way you use your time requires that you set some goals about what you want to be and do. Uncertainty breeds inactivity. Psychologists tell us that goals are the key to successful living. The reason more people are not successful is that they do not pursue specific goals. They simply shift from one activity to another without any focus or purpose, naively assuming that things will take care of themselves or will be taken care of by others.

Analyzing Your Time

Before you can determine how to spend your time differently, you should analyze how you spend it now. Exactly where does your day go? Surveys and observations of several thousand people suggest that the average day is divided into six major segments, as shown in Figure 12-1. Generally speaking, we have about two hours each day to do the various personal things that make life worth living. That's not much, but it gets worse. By their own account, most people waste at least two hours every day!

Those of us who work five days a week should theoretically have an additional twenty hours on the weekend for enriching our lives. However, many of us work more than forty hours each week. Executives, for instance, work from an average of almost sixty hours weekly to eighty hours a week and even more. Not surprisingly, weekends are lost. An evening off is a luxury. Sleep time gets cut dangerously short; meals are eaten too fast; tension mounts, and stress builds to dangerous levels. What better reason for learning to manage your time better? It's your life we're talking about!

Figure 12-1. Where does the day go?

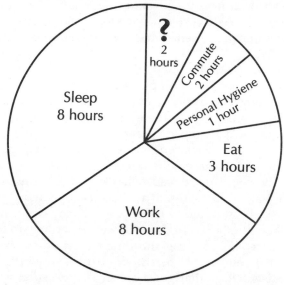

Most of us think that we know where our time goes, but unless we keep an exact record, we probably don't know. Countless studies show that most people can't remember exactly what they did only yesterday or the day before. If you really want to know yourself—and what you value—you must study yourself closely.

The two things that define you better than anything else is where you spend your time and where you spend your money. Most of us don't want to be accountable for either of these areas. Analyzing both your time and money expenditures, though, will provide a view of yourself that is difficult to obtain otherwise.

Keep Track of Time

For the next month, keep track of your personal time and what you do with it. Keep a record, too, of where you spend all your money during the month. Be honest with yourself. At the end of the month, summarize everything. Examine what percentage of your time is devoted to each activity and what things you spent your funds on. How much of your time and money is spent on "have-to's"? How much is spent on the things you want do? Question everything closely. Is it necessary? Does it add value to your life? What would happen if you eliminated it? Could you spend less time or money on it and still get acceptable results?

The answers may surprise you. You may discover that the "total you" is a lot different from what you think. For example, one of our friends swore she "hardly ever" watched TV in the evening. However, her time log revealed an average of sixteen hours weekly. The reality of that large amount of lost time drove her to make several positive changes.

If you are like our friend, you'll find your personal time analysis extremely valuable. It will help you break out of the personal activity traps that prevent you from achieving your goals. Seeing your life on paper is often a sobering experience.

Define Ideal Time

When you examine your goals, do not think exclusively of career goals or financial goals. Other aspects of your life—family, social activities, and so on—are important as well. If you want to be truly effective and satisfied with yourself, you must determine how to balance the various parts of your life. You must discover how to allocate your time to cover all those areas that are most important to you. Realize that the balance that is appropriate for you may not be appropriate for anyone else. This is a purely personal undertaking.

What people value most can be divided into seven broad areas: spiritual life, family or personal concerns, career, social life, physical development or health, mental development, and financial security. How do you distribute your time across these different areas? How much of your money is spent for each? We are not suggesting here that you should divide your time or money equally across these seven areas; nobody's life is so evenly divided. However, most people emphasize only two or three of these areas—without realizing it. A careful analysis will help you get a clearer picture of what you really value.

Before you undertake your time analysis, think about what you expect to find. Draw a circle and divide it into "pie" segments according to how you think you distribute your time in the seven different areas (see Figure 12-2). How much time each day do you spend on your career, your intellectual development, your family, and so on?

After you make your time analysis, draw another circle to indicate how you actually distribute your time. Now think about how you would *like* to spend your time. What are your most important goals? Considering the seven areas discussed, what do you wish your life looked like? Draw an "ideal" circle showing how you would like to spend your time. The difference between where you are now and where you would like to be is the source for possible goals.

Figure 12-2. Worksheet for allocating your day.

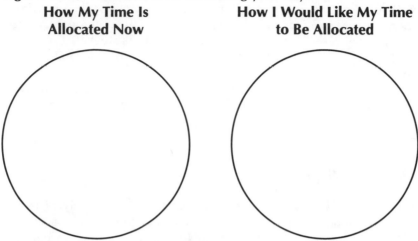

| How My Time Is Allocated Now | How I Would Like My Time to Be Allocated |

Most of us think very little about our goals. We respond or react to pressures from other people or things. But if you want to control your own time and life, you must decide what your goals are. No one can do this for you. And because you are likely to find what you are looking for, it is important that you pursue appropriate personal goals.

Setting Achievable Goals

Goals are far more than *dreams;* yet many of us use the two words interchangeably. We think of goals in the abstract—in terms of happiness, wealth, or fame. But goals mean something more. To have a goal means having a concrete objective, a well-clarified purpose. It means having something specific you wish to achieve. If you can determine what you want, you can probably find a way to obtain it.

Identify Your Goals

For example, instead of deciding that your goal is to "be rich," think about how much money would make you feel "rich" today. Is it $50,000, or $500,000, or $50 million? If your goal is to be a good family person, what exactly do you mean? Does that mean spending ten hours a week playing with your kids? Do you need to go out on the town with your spouse two evenings a week? If your goal is personal development, can you achieve it by attending four adult education classes a year? Exactly—specifically—what does your goal mean to you?

Goals should not only be specific and concrete; they should also be realistic. Finishing the Boston Marathon may be a realistic goal; winning it may not. Goals should make you stretch, but they should be attainable and measurable. Above all, they should be put in writing, with a time schedule for their completion. It is not easy to define a goal that meets all these criteria, but the effort is well worth it. The result is a goal that stimulates you, a goal that motivates you to begin pursuing it right away.

Try the following exercise to sharpen your goal-setting skills. Lay out seven sheets of paper. On each sheet list one of the seven major aspects of life discussed earlier: spiritual life, family or personal concerns, career, social life, physical development or health, mental development, and financial security. Now write down everything you can think of that you would like to accomplish in each area during your lifetime. Don't evaluate anything; just write down your thoughts. Try to fill each sheet of paper. Write quickly, but take as much time as you like. Reach back into your memory. Try to remember all the things you ever wanted to accomplish. The more ideas you write down, the better.

When you have listed everything you can think of, review all the items you have noted. Some of them are more important to you than others. Because you are after the best use of your time, and because you will not be able to do everything, you need to set priorities.

Set Priorities

Some of us find it difficult to set priorities in our personal life. It really isn't hard. Here is a simple but effective approach to establishing priorities. As you read over the seven lists of objectives you have prepared, rate them with an ABC system. Put an *A* beside those items that are very important to you. Put a *B* beside those that are moderately important, and put a *C* beside those that are least important. Try not to use the *B* as a cop-out; the exercise will become a useless long list of B priorities. Force yourself to decide between *A* or *C* whenever you can.

You now have a simple priority system. If you were to spend your personal time most effectively, you would concentrate on doing the A activities first and the B activities next, and you would forget about the C activities entirely.

Like most people, you probably have several A items on each list. If so, you need to refine your focus. Which of your A priorities are most important? Go through each sheet and indicate them A-1, A-2, A-3, and so forth, until all your A items are ranked.

Now look to see what item you have ranked A-1 on each sheet. You might list all the A-1 items on a separate sheet of paper and then rank-order them. In other words, the various aspects of your life are not equally important. Determine which ones are more important to you than others. In this way, you can be sure of focusing on the most important objectives first.

Do any of your objectives conflict? Many people find, for example, that they are torn between family and career. No matter how much they protest, in reality, their children always seem to come out second. It's hard to take your son to the ball game when you could be earning a bonus if you devoted the day to work. And, if you decide to work, you rationalize that the bonus enables your son to have advantages you didn't have. But your relationship with your son probably depends more on the quantity and quality of the time you spend with him than on his material well-being. There are no easy answers, just hard questions.

Review Your Time Analyses

Review your time analysis again. How many of the things you do actually relate to your A objectives? Are you spending time in a way that is consistent with achieving your A objectives, or do your activities lead somewhere else? You should devote some time to your A objectives each day—even if it is only a few minutes. Spend some time doing the things that are really important to you. Personal activity traps occur when your daily routine does not lead to your A objectives. For example, if your objective is to learn to plan the piano, don't fall into the activity trap of spending so much time dusting it that you never have time to play it. It's time to stop dusting and start playing.

Resolve to give up the C items in your life forever. Is TV really worth that much time? Are you sure you have to do all that housework? Why can't you play golf instead of cutting the grass? Did you really want to join the bowling league, or were you just unable to say no? Cutting out the C items and replacing them with A items can change your life. You're likely to become excited about living. The most interesting people to be around are those who are achieving things that are important to them. When you're focusing on your A objectives, it's impossible to have an apathetic, humdrum life.

We often get trapped into thinking that the C activities have to be done. This is not always the case. Remember Pareto's principle, the 80-20 rule. The 20 percent of the items accounting for 80 percent of the value in your life are probably related to your A objectives. The remaining 80 percent of the items accounting for 20 percent of the value in your life probably relate to the C activities you have deluded yourself into doing each day. If you want to be more satisfied with your personal life, learn to concentrate on the 20 percent of the items with high value. If you don't have time to work on your A objectives, it's because you are doing all those C activities, not because there isn't enough time.

If you are married, you and your spouse should undertake the lifetime objectives exercise separately. Each of you should determine the objectives that are important to you individually. When you each have your own list of A objectives, compare the items on both lists. There will probably be some conflict, so be prepared to negotiate and compromise. If you have children, let them participate in the process too.

The members of your family have a legitimate claim on some of your time. Many of your A objectives are likely to relate to family activities. When more than one person is involved, compromise is inevitable. Your challenge is to find a balance that will allow each family member to attain as many A objectives as possible.

Taking Action

Setting objectives in only the first step toward a more satisfying and fulfilling life. Your next task is to prepare an action plan for achieving your objectives. For example, if your goal is to improve your physical condition and you have decided that you need to jog twelve miles a week to achieve this goal, you must schedule a time to do your jogging—or it won't happen. Write it down and then do it!

Schedule

Scheduling is the best way to eliminate those vague, random activities that waste your time and lead you nowhere. If you want something to happen, you must make a place for it. You must carve out the time and space that your goal demands. Nothing happens unless you make it happen.

Because lifetime goals are usually complex and because it will probably take you some time to achieve them, it is helpful to break each goal down into subgoals. This will make your goals more believable and will motivate you to take the first step. Set a realistic target date for achieving each subgoal. Write down what you will gain by achieving that subgoal. Then move toward your larger goals by working on subgoals one step at a time. As you achieve your subgoals, you will gain a great deal of self-confidence and satisfaction. And all the while you will be gaining your important lifetime goals.

Do not be overly concerned if you do not have much time each day to devote to your goals. Even fifteen minutes a day can make a tremendous difference in your life. In fifteen minutes a day, you can learn a foreign language, trace your family history, learn to play a musical instrument, or read a good book. Fifteen minutes a day add up to over ninety hours each year. That's the equivalent of two full workweeks. Minutes do count. If you use them wisely, they can make a big difference in the quality of your life. Realize, of course, that as your situation changes, your goals may change. Different things may become more or less important to you. Your goals will change to reflect changes in your values, experiences, and aspirations.

Review Your Goal

Take time to review your long-range personal goals periodically. Your birthday is a good time to do this. Once a year reflect on who you are and who you want to be, what you'd like to accomplish in your life, and what things you find valuable. Share your thoughts with those who are important to you. Encourage them to improve the quality of their lives too.

If you really want to control your time, you cannot rely on luck. You must plan. You have often heard that "Failing to plan means planning to fail." Well, it's true! Plans for accomplishing lifetime objectives are usually long range. Plans for accomplishing daily objectives are short range. Over time, however, all those short-range daily goals should lead to your long-range goals. So, whether you are planning for tomorrow or for the rest of your life, the system is essentially the same: (1) Identify your objectives; (2) clarify your priorities; and (3) decide on your plan of action.

Controlling Your Time and Your Life

You can control your time and your life. In doing so, you will accomplish more, gain more satisfaction from the things you do, and feel more fulfilled. As your feelings of achievement, satisfaction, and fulfillment increase, the quality of your life increases. Your time is your life, and as you become more effective in managing your time, you create a better life for yourself.

Satisfaction lies in accomplishing the things that are really important. This is one of the secrets of success, as a time-conscious young friend of ours named Chuck found out. Chuck was an extremely gifted person, always eager to learn and involve himself in a new venture. He spent several years in the Air Force and traveled around the world. His inquisitive mind led him to investigate the wonders of mathematics and science, while his love of beauty called him to art and music. As he grew older, his mechanical abilities merged with his artistic soul and he found his vocation as a photographer.

But Chuck was no ordinary picture taker. True to his character, he approached his career with no holds barred. He was going to be the best photographer in the area, perhaps even in the state or the country. He advertised. He slaved. He ran to weddings. He raced to graduations. He took portraits of anyone who could find his number in the telephone book. He was consumed by his job. His photos were signed "By Charles." He had arrived.

One day, almost by accident, "Charles" found his way into our course on time management while he was taking pictures for a yearbook. As he snapped away at the various participants, he listened to the discussion of time. The discussion aroused his attention and he asked the instructor if he might have one of the workbooks.

"Charles" took the workbook home. One day when a scheduled wedding was canceled, he decided to read it. He was fascinated by the content, stimulated by the idea of applying the concepts to his own life, and horrified when he did a time analysis and saw what he had become. He was a workaholic! Cheryl, his wife, and his two children were nearly strangers. He had no associates or friends outside the photography business; he had not given his church a minute's time in five years; his former interests in math, music, science, and art had become nothing but a memory.

He vowed to change. He announced to his wife that things would be different from now on. Her reply? "Sure!"

But today, Cheryl is amazed and happy. "Charles" has turned back into the Chuck she married, and he is even more fascinating than before. By applying time-management principles to his work, Chuck has made his photography studio more successful than ever. Equally important to Chuck and his family, his private life is also a success. He knows his goals and priorities. He also lives them. He spends hours each day deeply involved with the family he loves very much. He plans for tomorrow but lives for today—in the ways that are important to him.

Like Chuck, you should demand as much return on your personal time as you do on your business time. If you don't like the return on your personal time investment, change the way you spend your time. Quality of life is a function of what you do, when you do it, whom you do it with, and what you accomplish in the process. Through proper application of time-management techniques, you can be more productive on the job than ever before—and you can gain more personal time in the process. By applying the same techniques to your personal life, you can begin to achieve many of your dreams.

Look Back

If your life has been too hectic, if you have been totally absorbed in your work to the neglect of other aspects of your life, it's time to take a new look at your priorities. Consider the following questions:

1. The last time I spent a quiet evening at home (do I remember it?), did my spouse and children look at me suspiciously? Did they know what to do with me? If they didn't, did they care? Have I been gone so much of the time that my family has learned to live nicely "around" my presence?
2. Have I been promising myself that I'm going to "get in shape" soon? Do I continually say that someday I'll start running, swimming, or playing tennis? Did I forget to have a medical or dental checkup last year? (Some doctors claim it's all down-hill after age 26!)
3. When was the last time I spent the evening with friends? Do I continue to see people here and there but never get beyond saying, "We'll have to have you over sometime?" When I do have people over, am I too tired to enjoy the evening? Am I still thinking about my work?
4. Am I honestly in control of my life? If I could write the script of the life I'd like to lead, what would it look like? What choices do I have to make *now* to live the life I desire?

Learn From Your Regrets

A number of years ago, an elderly man wrote to *Guideposts* magazine expressing his regrets. He said that if he had his life to live over, he would relax more and not take so many things as seriously. He would take more chances, climb more mountains, and swim more rivers. He'd ride more merry-go-rounds. He'd pick more daisies. If you could go back and live your life over, what would you change?

We all have regrets, according to Professor Richard Kinnier of Arizona State University. Professor Kinnier has asked hundreds of people about what they regret. His studies show the most common regret was not being a better student, not studying more. Other common regrets reported by Professor Kinnier include not being more assertive, not having more self-discipline, not taking more risks, not spending quality time with our families. And one surprise showed up in Professor Kinnier's research. All things considered, money appears to be insignificant in the grand scheme of things.

Regrets are just part of life. Having regrets is not necessarily bad, unless you let them be. In a way, regrets are unavoidable, no matter what you do. They often arise because what you value changes as you grow older. Studying is probably a good example. When you were young, you were more interested in having fun than in studying. Years later, you come to see the value of study. Then, you wish you could go back and live your earlier life over with the values and knowledge gained in your later years. This, of course, can never be.

There are two lessons we can learn from regrets. The first point is that some regrets are irreversible. We need to think carefully about what is really important. We can't go back and play with our children after they are grown.

The second point is that some regrets are partially reversible. If you regret not going to college, you can always go later. However, you can't go back to where you were.

Whether our regrets are reversible or irreversible, we should never let regrets stymie us. We should look back and learn from the past, but we must always realize that we are free to change the future. Life has one direction, and that is straight ahead.

One point we've tried to emphasize throughout this book is that good time management is a highly subjective process. It's your life. What do you want to do with it? If you don't know, find out. The world is waiting for you when you do. It is pointless to attack life in a desperate frenzy. You'll never get out alive! Relax your way through. Try to make the world just a little bit better because you were there. Your time will be well spent if you do.

Scoring Guide for Chapter Twelve Quiz				
	SA	**MA**	**U**	**MD**	**SD**
1.	5	4	3	2	1
2.	1	2	3	4	5
3.	5	4	3	2	1
4.	5	4	3	2	1

Thirteen
Drawing Your Personal Time-Management Profile

In this chapter, we'll take a look at the overall picture. When we're finished, you'll be able to see our own personal Time-Management Profile . . . in graphic display!

Many people see time management as a rather narrow, single issue. For some of us it only means making lists or being more efficient. However, we believe that managing time is multidimensional and reaches into every aspect of your life. Throughout this book, we've been exploring these various dimensions.

Here's a summary of the major time-management aspects we've discussed up to this point. For each aspect, we've suggested a critical question for you to consider.

Major Aspect	*Critical Question*
Dilemma	I never seem to have enough time, yet I have all the time there is. The problem is not a shortage of time, but how I choose to use the time available. How do I choose to use the time I have?
Goals	How do I clarify my goals and decide what to focus on?
Priorities	How do I decide what's important, what to do first, and what to let wait?
Analysis	How much do I know about my time habits, where I spend my time, and whether or not my behavior is consistent with my goals?
Plans	How do I plan my work and my time?
Schedules	How do I schedule time for doing the most important tasks?

Major Aspect	*Critical Question*
Paperwork	How do I go about streamlining the detail part of my job?
Interruptions	How do I systematically work at eliminating or reducing interruptions?
Travel	How do I manage my time when I am on trips?
Procrastination	How do I overcome my tendency to put things off?
Stress	How do I handle stress and tension in my life?
Balance	How well is my time balanced across all parts of my life?

Discovering Your Time-Mastery Level

We've presented the Time-Management Profile in pieces. Chapter by chapter, we've asked you to assess your normal behavior patterns. Each chapter dealt with a different aspect of time management. At the beginning of each chapter, you indicated how much your normal behavior matched the statements listed. At the end of the chapter, there was a scale for scoring your responses. If you haven't done this, please go back and do it now.

Now, simply transfer your total score from each of the chapter quizzes to the section below:

Total Score on
Chapter Quizzes

Goals
(Chapter Two, page 9; scoring guide on
page 20)   _____

Priorities
(Chapter Three, page 21; scoring guide
on page 31)   _____

Analysis
(Chapter Four, page 32; scoring guide
on page 50)   _____

Plans
(Chapter Five, page 51; scoring guide
on page 67)   _____

Total Score on
Chapter Quizzes

Schedules
   (Chapter Six, page 68; scoring guide on
   page 84)   _____

Paperwork
   (Chapter Seven, page 85; scoring guide
   on page 101)   _____

Interruptions
   (Chapter Eight, page 102; scoring
   guide on page 112)   _____

Travel
   (Chapter Nine, page 113; scoring guide
   on page 124)   _____

Procrastination
   (Chapter Ten, page 125; scoring guide
   on page 135)   _____

Stress
   (Chapter Eleven, page 136; scoring
   guide on page 150)   _____

Balance
   (Chapter Twelve, page 151; scoring
   guide on page 163)   _____

Total score
   Add all chapter quizzes' scores
   together   _____

To find your overall time-mastery level, compare your total score to the time mastery levels shown below. The higher your score, the greater the indication that you have mastered good time management.

Total Score	Time-Mastery Level
44–62	I
63–97	II
98–167	III
168–202	IV
203–220	V

Remember, though, that your score on the Time-Management Profile is only a number. It represents conditions as they exist now. It's the result of habits you've developed in the past. However, it does not determine what you will be or do in the future. That's up to you.

The purpose of the Time-Management Profile is to help you discover your personal time-management strengths and weaknesses. It can be valuable in helping you decide how to improve. It can help pinpoint which improvements would help you most. Whether or not you choose to change depends on you. However, if you do choose to improve, the Time-Management Profile can be an excellent guide to help you become a top time master.

Accentuate the Positive

Most people, when they examine their scores, tend to focus on what's wrong. Don't do this. Instead, look for what's right. For example, go back and look for every statement where your response scored five points. Those are your strengths! You're doing something right. Feel good about them. Congratulate yourself!

To improve, build on your strengths. Start with what you're already good at, and add to it. Consider which improvements would help you most. Focus on a few things at a time. Master these, then move on to a few more. Don't tackle more than you can handle and you will increase your chances for success. Remember, "Yard by yard, life is hard; but inch by inch, life's a cinch."

Study the statements carefully. Look for patterns. Think about the implications for your job. Which items are more critical than others? Which ones can you control? Which ones would help you most if you were to improve on them? Think carefully about where to focus first.

Graphing Your Time-Management Profile

The next step is to graph your Time-Management Profile. Transfer your score for each category above to the graph below. On the scale to the right of each category name, circle the number that matches your score for that category. Connect all eleven points on the scale into a continuous graph line for easier viewing. Figure 13-1 illustrates a completed Profile graph.

Figure 13-1.   Sample time-management profile graph.

Your Personal Time-Management Profile

	I	II	III	IV	V
Chapter Two: Goals	4 5	6 7 8	9 10 11 12 13 14 15	16 17 18	19 20
Chapter Three: Priorities	4 5	6 7 8	9 10 11 12 13 14 15	16 17 18	19 20
Chapter Four: Analysis	4 5	6 7 8	9 10 11 12 13 14 15	16 17 18	19 20
Chapter Five: Plans	4 5	6 7 8	9 10 11 12 13 14 15	16 17 18	19 20
Chapter Six: Schedules	4 5	6 7 8	9 10 11 12 13 14 15	16 17 18	19 20
Chapter Seven: Paperwork	4 5	6 7 8	9 10 11 12 13 14 15	16 17 18	19 20
Chapter Eight: Interruptions	4 5	6 7 8	9 10 11 12 13 14 15	16 17 18	19 20
Chapter Nine: Travel	4 5	6 7 8	9 10 11 12 13 14 15	16 17 18	19 20
Chapter Ten: Procrastination	4 5	6 7 8	9 10 11 12 13 14 15	16 17 18	19 20
Chapter Eleven: Stress	4 5	6 7 8	9 10 11 12 13 14 15	16 17 18	19 20
Chapter Twelve: Balance	4 5	6 7 8	9 10 11 12 13 14 15	16 17 18	19 20

The dotted lines divide the graph into five time-mastery levels, beginning with Level I on the left and proceeding through Level V on the right. The higher your score, the more you have mastered that aspect of managing time. Your goal, then, is to move your scores as far to the right as possible . . . to Level IV or Level V.

You will probably notice that your time-mastery level for some categories is either higher or lower than the overall time-mastery level you calculated above. This is normal. It simply means that you are better at some aspects of managing time than you are at others.

This graph is another way to help you decide where to begin your time-management improvement program. What are the implications of the pattern you see in your chart? Which categories are most critical for your job? Which categories can you control most or change most easily? Start with the categories that you believe will help you the most.

From time to time, retake the Time-Management Profile, and compare your new results to earlier results. Notice how you have improved. Some people even like to graph their improvement curves. It can't hurt, and it may help motivate you to keep going.

How to Get Copies of the Time-Management Profile

An expanded version of the Time-Management Profile—with fourteen categories—is available from Time Management Center. The Profile is self-scoring and takes only a few minutes to complete. It is a valuable tool, whether used individually or in groups. For instance, the Time-Management Profile can be used in training seminars or in staff meetings. By adding individual scores together, you could even develop group or department profiles.

For more information about the Time-Management Profile, please contact:

Dr. Merrill Douglass
Time Management Center
1401 Johnson Ferry Road, Suite 328–D6
Marietta, GA 30062
Tel: 404-973-3977

Time Management Center also can provide workbooks, booklets, cassette tapes, and various training materials. In addition, we can present one of our highly acclaimed Time-Management Seminars for your group. For more information about our resource materials or our seminars, please contact the Time Management Center.

Fourteen
Creating Positive Success Habits

When you choose a habit, you also choose the results of that habit.

Zig Ziglar

We control habits, but habits control destinies. Clearly, a good part of our lives is spent in habitual fashion. Most of our daily behavior follows a pattern and a routine; psychologists say that as much as 80 to 90 percent of our actions are habitual. Habits by definition are behaviors that have been performed so often that they have become automatic. This means that habitual behaviors operate just below our consciousness threshold. When we are preoccupied—or acting habitually—we are not free to manage our time. We are simply not as alert as when we are acting nonhabitually. Managing time requires accurate observation of what is taking place.

We sometimes assume that habits are always bad. This is not true. Many habits are quite beneficial. If we had to consciously decide on everything we did during the day, life would become quite unbearable. Once we learn to do something well, automatic habit control is a blessing.

For example, you bathe, dress, eat, and do dozens of similar routines every day. The advantage, of course, is that you can devote your attention to other things while you carry out the task at hand. Your body continues on in the same routine fashion as long as nothing unexpected happens. If an unexpected event does occur, your mind instantly focuses on what you are doing and you are no longer behaving habitually.

Driving an automobile illustrates this point well. As long as the roads, traffic, and car function predictably, you can drive "on automatic"—with your mind a million miles away. However, if a child darts across your path, you must summon all your skills as a driver to save the child's life—and often your own as well.

However, in general, you may want to reduce some of your habitual behavior in order to use time more effectively. If you spend a large percentage of your day in habitual routines, you are probably not using time as well as you could. The best way to begin reducing habitual behavior is to discover your present habit patterns. As you uncover these patterns, the need for change becomes obvious, and you become more motivated to make the change. You will begin to discover which habit patterns are beneficial and which are detrimental.

Changing Your Habits

No one can force you to change, of course. But if you wish to improve the way you spend your time, to gain more control over it, to achieve better results from it, unquestionably you will have to change some habits. No one can change your behavior for you. You must do it yourself. This doesn't mean that other people will be totally out of the picture. Certain associates may play a crucial role in your efforts. Practice, however, will be up to you. Others may help to reinforce your new behaviors, but it is you who must, voluntarily, undertake them.

Recognize Your Habit Patterns

Habits are often difficult to change because they are interconnected. A single action becomes a cue for some other action, which in turn may be a cue for still another behavior. In this way, we develop habit sequences that form a vigorous mode of patterned behavior.

Everything is related to everything else. Events do not stand as isolated instances in our lives; they are inextricably related to other times, places, and things. A change in one part of our life, therefore, has a direct impact on other parts of our life as well.

Identify Cues

Some of us are too casual in our approach to changing habits. We mistakenly think that change is easy and that it's "all in the head." It's true that it's all in your head, but that's also the problem! You have to change your head. You need to uncover things that cue your behavior. Psychologists recognized many years ago that behavior is a response to a stimulus. We get hungry at the sight of delicious food. We desire a cigarette along with our drink. We want a snack when we watch television in the evening. Cues are trigger events. When a cue occurs, we respond habitually.

Once you recognize the trigger event, you have three ways to approach habit change. You can change the trigger event, change the response to the trigger event, or change both. For instance, you could cut down on fattening snacks if you stopped watching television. Or you could learn to munch on celery sticks. You could also learn to munch on celery sticks while doing something other than watching television.

Manipulate Your Environment

Your efforts at change can be improved if you seek ways to manipulate your environment to reinforce the new behavior. For instance, suppose you are a heavy smoker and want to stop smoking. One way to put yourself in a supportive environment would be to take a wilderness vacation for two weeks with nonsmokers. Take no cigarettes with you, and make sure your vacation site is miles from the nearest store. Under those conditions it will be much easier for you to stop smoking. By the time you return from your trip, you should be well launched into your new pattern of not smoking. You must still safeguard your smoke-free status, however, because the old cues in your environment will continue to have power over you. But with a strong start you're more likely to continue.

Any change in your environment will facilitate a change in behavior. Try rearranging your office. Move the furniture around. Put desk items in different drawers. Reorganize the file drawer. Use different routes for traveling within the office building. Come in and out of different doors from the usual ones. Do anything that is different, and you will raise your general awareness of what is taking place around you. As your awareness level goes up, you will be in a better position to recognize and change your habit patterns.

Launching New Behaviors

According to the best research done on altering personal behavior, the following crucial seven conditions must be present:

1. Desire
2. Knowledge
3. Planning
4. Visualizing
5. Action

6. Support
7. Evaluation

No change will take place without the desire to make a change. How much do you really want to change your work habits to function more effectively? Desire is the key to success or failure. If you have a strong desire, you will probably initiate many changes. If you have only a little desire, you will only change a few small things.

We want to stress how important it is to work through *all* seven steps. Many people fail, hard as they try, because they complete only the first three steps, but stop short of steps four through seven. These last steps haven't been emphasized as frequently as the first three, but they are the secret that adds punch to the initial ones.

One part of us likes things as they are even if they are bothersome and we complain a great deal. We're unworried and unconcerned about change. Another part of us is demanding more. It wants greater accomplishment. At any time, most of us experience some conflict between these two parts of ourselves: the one part not wanting change and the other part demanding change. The winning half says a great deal about whether or not we actually change.

Desire

In order to change long-established habits, you must *want* to change. What we suggest is not always simple, or at least easy, and change is not for everyone. All the suggestions in the world are worthless if you do not want to change. And changing the way you use your time is largely a voluntary effort. You cannot force others to use their time well, and they cannot force you to use your time well. The "want to" must come from inside.

We're not exactly sure where desire comes from. It has something to do with satisfaction and comfort zones. The more satisfied you are, the less you desire to change. But with mounting dissatisfaction there is a tension toward fixing the problem. Unfortunately, many of us are only a little dissatisfied but not enough to jar us out of our comfort zone. We become so comfortable with our old discomforts that we often put up with any disadvantage as an acceptable alternative to initiating change. We would rather put up with our problems than change our habits.

Knowledge

Desiring is the first step, but it is not sufficient. Once you desire to change, you must understand what needs to be changed and how to go about changing it. Knowledge is essential. Knowledge comes from analyzing some things, discovering your habit patterns, increasing your awareness, and observing what you actually do.

It is best when you can pinpoint the precise behaviors you wish to change. In what conditions do they occur? What triggers the behavior? What assumptions support your present behavior? How does your personality style affect your behavior patterns? The more you know about what you do, when you do it, and why you do it, the easier it will be for you to change.

Planning

The next step is to create a plan for accomplishing the change. What exactly do you intend to accomplish? What activities are needed? What are you willing to do? When will you do each step? What obstacles are likely to arise? What personal shortcomings will get in your way? How will you handle these issues?

Most of us would be reasonably good at planning if we set aside the time for it. Unfortunately, many of us barge ahead without a plan, assuming that planning is necessary for others but not for us. We soon discover our mistake. With a good, well-thought-out plan, the actual changing is much easier.

Carefully define the new habits you wish to develop. It may help to write a description of the new habit you plan to create. Draw a line from top to bottom on a sheet of paper, dividing it into two halves. On the left-hand side, describe the habit you wish to change. On the right-hand side, describe the new habit you plan to adopt. Describe everything you know about both the old and new habits.

Action plans work best when you are accountable to someone else. When you finish your action plan, date it and sign your name to it. Tomorrow, give a copy of your action plan to someone important to you, and ask that person to meet with you weekly so you can review your progress together. Then, get started, because the first weekly checkpoint isn't very far away.

People who know what they want suddenly find their life filled with opportunities. A compelling purpose makes it easier to develop the discipline required to build good habits. And good habits will propel you toward your goal.

Visualizing

Once you understand what needs to be changed and how to go about changing it, you must be able to visualize yourself under the new condition. You must be able to see yourself living and working in the new manner before you can change. This works as well for you as it does for professional athletes. Many Olympic athletes talk at length about how they perform in their minds thousands of times before they actually accomplish the feat on the field. Noted golfer Jack Nicklaus says the ability to review and correct mistakes in his mind is the key to winning tournaments. But if you can only see the old conditions, you cannot create the new ones.

This was driven home vividly to us several years ago when our son was learning to play golf. As he began to play, he had a very negative picture of himself as a golfer. He made lots of mistakes, grumbling and complaining all the way. He kept telling himself that he would never learn to do it right. His mental picture was unsuccessful. In his mind, he could only see himself making mistakes. It was not until he was able to visualize himself doing it right that he began to make progress.

It works the same for you. For instance, if you see your lack of assertiveness as a major problem in controlling your time, you will never change until you can see yourself acting in a more assertive manner. If you want to implement a quiet hour or conduct productive meetings, you must first be able to see these happening in your mind. Once you can see yourself successfully doing the new behavior, the next step, action, is relatively easy.

Action

Begin the new behavior as strongly as possible. Do it with gusto! Tell everyone you can about the new habit you intend to develop. Set up a routine to go with your habit. Put up signs or pictures to remind you of the new behavior. Remember the importance of cues, how one action leads to another action. If possible, change your environment to upset the old cues, and provide fresh soil for rooting your new habit.

In the beginning, your new behavior will not feel comfortable. It will not reflect what you would "naturally" do in a given situation. To keep yourself going, you may need to remind yourself daily of the benefits you will derive from the new behavior.

To begin strongly means to do it now, *immediately!* Practice the new behavior even when you don't need to. Suppose that your new behavior pattern involves learning to remember people's names. You might try using a person's name frequently in conversation. If you don't meet new people regularly on your job, you can practice this polite form of "name calling" on your friends and colleagues. If you develop the habit of using names frequently when you talk to people, you will be more comfortable using a stranger's name in conversation. Through this practice, you will begin to shape your behavior and become a master of new names.

Use every opportunity to practice the new behavior. No matter how strongly you are committed to the new habit, it will not become yours until you actually use the behavior. Seek opportunities to use it. Arrange your schedule so you adopt the new behavior more frequently than normal in the beginning. Do everything you can to practice the new behavior until it becomes a habit.

Never deviate from the new behavior until the new habit is firmly established. You will be tempted many times to do things in the old way. Resist these temptations. Some people rationalize deviations by saying, "Just this once won't matter." The truth is that each deviation matters a great deal. Every time you deviate you must start all over again. The more you attempt to start over, the harder it is to change.

How long does it take to replace one habit with another? This, of course, depends on many considerations. However, many of your work-related habits can be successfully changed in three to thirty days. In other words, if you consistently practice the new behavior, without deviation, for three days to thirty days, it will become your predominant response pattern. At that point, you have replaced the old habit with a new one.

Support

Some habits are rather mild, and you can change them with only a modest amount of effort. Some habits, though, are particularly hard to change. They may have a strong emotional component, or they may have been formed in early childhood. Changing these habits will be tough.

Psychologists who study habit change point out that most of us do not make any significant changes without a support group. We need the encouragment and empathy of other people. It often helps if those other people have gone through a similar change themselves. They are living proof that it can be done.

Find or develop a support group to help you through the change. Convince someone else to make the same change, so you can go through the process together. Set up a simple accountability system with a buddy. Meet regularly with your support group to talk about problems and progress.

Two things seem to help when considering a support group. First, you want people who will be supportive, not critical. Second, you want people who can affirm you and hold you to your commitment at the same time. Psychologists call this tough love. They won't accept glib excuses for nonconforming behavior. Because they expect great things of you, you also expect great things of yourself.

Evaluation

Periodically take a look to see how things are progressing. Do this with your support group, and do this for yourself. How far have you come? What successes have you had? What is working out well?

Don't get caught up in how far you still have to go. Rejoice in the progress you have made. Feel good about your successes, and it will motivate you to continue. Feel depressed about what you haven't achieved yet and you will probably quit.

Using Work Segmentation

One good approach for building good habits at work is called work segmentation. Examine the different kinds of work you do in the office. If you arrange to do particular jobs in specific spots, you will concentrate better and avoid distractions. For example, you might sit at your credenza for all telephone calls and write all your financial reports at your desk. Use another work table for handling general correspondence. Do all your reading on one of the chairs at the side of your desk. Segment your job in as many ways as possible so that you have a particular place to do each kind of work. Then, whenever you approach a particular work area, you will automatically start thinking about the kind of tasks you normally perform there.

If you can do each task at a specific time, the arrangement will be even better. For example, set aside a time for making phone calls; then go to the credenza to handle your calls. If you are interrupted and must do something else, switch to the appropriate location. If you begin to think about other things, get up and move for a few moments, then come back. Think of yourself as a television series: same time, same place, same content.

Of course, there are some disadvantages to this approach. When you have developed the habit of working on an activity in a specific location, it will be more difficult to perform that task in another location. If conditions change sufficiently, though, you can always recondition yourself to work at a different location.

Another dimension of work segmentation is to use airplanes, waiting rooms, and other travel locations as extensions of your office.

For example, if you fly a great deal, you might set aside certain kinds of work to be done only on plane trips. If possible, sit in the same seat on each trip and do similar kinds of work when in the air. Before long, the minute you sit down you will begin thinking about the kinds of work you generally do in that location. The trip will be less boring and you will have extended the time available for accomplishing important results.

Defining Success

Success is a powerful word, with strong connotations. We all want to succeed, no matter how we define success. It's the desire for success that often leads people to consider improving their time-management skills. Regardless of what motivates people to improve their time skills, the end result is always the same: Using them better leads to greater success, however success is defined. But how you define success can make a difference, because your motivation is closely linked with your definition.

Defining success is the first step in achieving success. People who don't have a personal definition for success feel less successful and earn less money. They are also less satisfied with their careers and their lives.

Personal Selling Power, the sales and marketing newsletter, once asked executives to describe what success meant to them personally. Responses fell into four categories.

1. Success means owning material possessions such as houses, cars, or airplanes.
2. Success means experiencing particular feelings such as feeling satisfied or happy.
3. Success means achieving goals, the process of getting from one point to the next. Respondents set goals and then achieved them.
4. Success is seen as a personal mission. Each of us has some mission in life, and success means finding and fulfilling that mission.

Differences between the four group definitions are easy to see. But does it really matter? Experience suggests that the first three groups often run into serious motivational problems. Material possessions never satisfy long, moods and feelings are nebulous, and even goals can seem meaningless after a while. People in group four seem to have a deeper foundation. Possessions, feelings, and goals all take on new meanings when measured by a life mission.

Defining a Personal Mission Statement

For most, this book is probably a what-to-do book. However, you can't effectively decide what to do until you first decide what to be. Strong companies have corporate statements, from which flow their strategies and goals. Individuals, too, should have personal mission statements, from which flow personal strategies and personal goals.

Creating a personal mission statement is not easy. Very few people have even thought about a personal mission for their life. But those who have actually worked one out are the most exciting, satisfied, fulfilled people you'll ever meet. They have found the way to be truly happy, and you want to find that way too.

Your personal life mission concerns your character more than it concerns your accomplishments. It focuses directly on your roles, relationships, and responsibilities. This is where you really figure out who you are and why you are here. As you strive to work out your mission statement, carefully consider your relationships with God, spouse, children, friends, community, employers, and self. What kind of person do you really want to be? What should the sum total of your life add up to? Write out your rough ideas, then edit and refine them.

Goals and activities (what to do) will naturally flow out of your definition of mission (what to be) because you will want to do those things that will help you fulfill your mission. You will soon find major changes in your life. Instead of a bunch of loose days randomly collected and pieced together, you will see your Life's Direction. All the odd pieces will miraculously fit together, revealing a beautiful whole. It is when you have this kind of focus that the true value of time-management skills and techniques becomes apparent.

Defining a personal mission in life and developing it are not easy tasks. But, then, success is not something that happens by accident. Not everyone who wants to be successful will be. People who are successful have usually *earned* their success one way or another.

Understanding Success

Hard work alone will not make us successful. The willingness to work hard may be a big part of our success, but it is only one factor. Many of us work hard and never succeed. Some of the most obviously qualified fail, and some with tremendous handicaps make it. Clearly, something besides hard work accounts for the difference between success and failure.

Earl Nightingale points out the secret for success in his cassette tape message "The Common Denominator of Success" (Chicago: Nightingale-Conant Corporation, 1978). He says that the secret for anyone who has ever been successful at anything is to form the habit of doing what failures don't want to do. Success, therefore, is "unnatural"; it cannot be achieved by following our "natural" instincts, habits, or preferences.

What are these things that failures don't like to do and that successful people are willing to do? According to Nightingale, they are the same things no one likes to do. For example, most people don't like to keep time logs, but the most successful time managers keep them routinely.

Then why do some people do them while others don't? Because successful people want to achieve their goals. Successful people are motivated by pleasing results and will do whatever they have to do to achieve them. Failures, on the other hand, are motivated by pleasing methods and will accept whatever results are possible by doing only what they feel like doing.

Doing the right things part of the time is not good enough. Successful people form the *habit* of doing the right things—all the time. Good time management is not easy; it requires more than a dab of self-discipline. Disciplined people do what they know they should do, whether or not they feel like it. They live their lives on the basis of decisions, not feelings.

Since success is not a natural state, we will have to change to be successful. We must set our sights higher. The *Christopher's Bulletin* ("Christopher's News Notes," October 1977) printed an American Indian legend about a brave who found an eagle's egg and put it into the nest of a prairie chicken. All his life, this changeling eagle—thinking he was a prairie chicken—did what prairie chickens did. He scratched in the dirt for seeds and insects to eat. He clucked and cackled. And he flew in a brief flurry of wings and feathers no more than a few feet off the ground. After all, that's how a prairie chicken was supposed to fly.

Years passed. The changeling eagle grew older. One day he saw a magnificent bird far above him in the cloudless sky. Hanging with graceful majesty on powerful wind currents, the bird soared with scarcely a beat of its strong golden wings.

"What a beautiful bird!" said the changeling eagle to his neighbor. "What is it?"

"That's an eagle, the chief of birds," the neighbor clucked. "But don't give it a second thought. You could never be like him."

So the changeling eagle never gave it a second thought. And he died thinking he was a prairie chicken.

It is all too easy to go through life thinking you are a prairie chicken when you might really be an eagle. By doing so you short-change yourself and everyone else around you. Be what you are. But be all that you can be. Don't settle for failure when you can have success. How you view yourself plays a vital role in how you choose to spend your time—and your life. Don't settle for less when you could have more.

Success Is a Habit

Nothing underscores the importance of habit more potently than this old American Indian proverb. Read it carefully, and think about what it means in your life.

> *Plant a thought, harvest an act.*
> *Plant an act, harvest a habit.*
> *Plant a habit, harvest a character.*
> *Plant a character, harvest a destiny.*

Habits are the basis for success. People form habits, but habits form futures. If you don't for your habits consciously, you will form them unconsciously. Unconscious habits are seldom as good as conscious ones. Either way, we are the product of our habits. As Zig Ziglar puts it, what we are is simply the sum of the habits that control us.

Time use is a habit. To improve, you must resolve to change your present habits. Of course, any resolution you make will not be worth much unless you keep it. You must stick to your resolution day in and day out until it becomes a habit—until one day you become a different person in a different world, until you have become the master of your likes and dislikes, until you have formed the habit of success.

Our purpose in writing this book was to provide the concepts, techniques, and motivation you need to improve the way you use your time. Commit yourself to action now, but don't expect miracles. Don't expect a sudden, dramatic turnaround. The habits that control you were not developed overnight. Change is not likely to occur overnight, either. The good news, though, is that you can change.

If we have been successful, you now know what to do to take charge of your time and your life. But knowledge is not enough because knowledge without action is impotent. Ultimately, to master time—or anything else—you must act. An ancient Chinese proverb—translated rather loosely—says it well: "A man must sit on a chair with his mouth open for a very long time before a roast duck flies in."

Commit yourself to success. Start where you are. Stop dreaming about tomorrow and start living today. If you can't find big time chunks, start with little time chunks. Act on the things you fear. Behave like the kind of person you would like to be, and you'll become that kind of person.

Remember that your success in managing time relates to your purpose in life and your commitment to that purpose. Examine your purpose carefully and make it as large as you can. Big purposes make big people. Remember, too that you can never succeed beyond the purpose to which you are willing to surrender yourself. And that surrender is never complete until you have formed the habit of doing things that failures don't like to do.

It's All Up to You

Most of us have discovered that there is a big difference between knowing what to do and doing it. We know the bridge between the two is called self-discipline, but we can't seem to cross it. Yet self-discipline is the significant difference between winners and losers. It is the difference between those who dream and those who achieve.

Self-discipline is the key to personal freedom. It paroles us from the prison of our habits and releases us to fulfill our lives. In a world where we often feel we control nothing individually, self-discipline helps us define that part of the world where we *can* make a difference.

Where do we find that golden key known as self-discipline? Philosophers and poets, inventors and executives have searched for it throughout the centuries. They can tell us only that it comes from within. We must find it for ourselves. We are the only ones who can unlock our potential and make time-management techniques work for us.

There are no six easy steps to becoming disciplined. Self-discipline is a mental process. Consider the following:

> Just about + self-discipline = Success!
> Planning + self-discipline = Achievement!
> Hoping + self-discipline = A winner!

The point? Those of us who dream and wish, those of us who aspire to anything great, those of us who want to become more than we are—we are only one step away. Without that step, we fail; but with that step we succeed. That one, all-important step is self-discipline.

Our part is over. It's now your turn. It's all up to you. What are you going to do? All it takes is belief and action. Can *you* do it? Henry Ford claimed that "whether you think you can, or whether you think you can't, you're right." Which destiny will you choose for yourself?

Remember: "If you're unhappy with the results of your present habits but you keep on doing what you've always done, you'll just get more of what you've already got! That spells d-i-s-s-a-t-i-s-f-a-c-t-i-o-n. Habits are the backbone of good time management. Take good care of your habits, and your habits will take good care of you.

Fifteen
Tips for Becoming a
Top Time Master

We appreciate your interest in learning to manage time better. We're also grateful that you purchased this book. We sincerely hope that it has helped you improve your time-management skills. In summary, here are thirty-nine tips for mastering your time.

1. Develop a statement of your life mission.
2. Clarify your goals. Focus on results, not just activities.
3. Be sure projects have priorities, due dates, and time estimates.
4. Review your long-range goals daily.
5. Use priority codes that indicate both importance and urgency. Concentrate on the important issues. Don't worry about trivia.
6. Ask yourself if what you are doing is helping you reach your goals. If not, switch to something else that will help.
7. Record and analyze how you actually spend your time. Find out what you do, when you do it, and why you do it. Ask yourself what would happen if you didn't do it. If the answer is "nothing," then stop doing it.
8. Make sure your first hour at work is a productive hour.
9. Strive for continual improvement in everything you do. Look for ways to work smarter, not harder.
10. Eliminate recurring crises from your life. Find out why things keep going wrong. Learn to proact instead of always reacting. Take time to do it right the first time, so you won't have to waste time doing it over.
11. Plan your time. Write out a plan for each week. Ask yourself what you hope to accomplish by the end of the week and what activities will be necessary to achieve those results. Consider how much time you will need, and set your priorities.

12. Meet regularly with others to coordinate plans, priorities, and activities.
13. Make your to-do list for tomorrow before you leave today.
14. Schedule the most important activities. Scheduled activities have a better chance of working out right.
15. Allow flexibility in your schedule for the unexpected things that you can't control.
16. Block out quiet time every day.
17. Be gracious with people but firm with time. Learn to respond appropriately and say NO when you should.
18. Try to eliminate at least one time waster every week.
19. Develop a strategy for handling and avoiding interruptions.
20. Bunch things together so you won't interrupt others so much during the day.
21. Make sure meetings are productive.
22. Develop a system for sorting and scheduling your paperwork.
23. Use tickler files to keep track of all the details.
24. Analyze paperwork and look for ways to eliminate it, simplify it, and streamline it.
25. Keep the clutter under control, and you'll work more efficiently and feel better too.
26. Show people you respect their time by developing the on-time habit: Be on time, be prepared, deliver work on time.
27. Look for ways to save time for others. Promote team time management.
28. Take time to provide clear instructions and complete information.
29. Ask people you work with how you waste their time and how you could help them get better results.
30. Practice the Golden Rule: Treat others the way you would like to be treated.
31. Take time to be a good listener. It saves lots of time and prevents many problems.
32. Learn to delegate effectively, and don't try to do everything yourself.
33. Conquer procrastination. Change your do-it-later urge into a do-it-now habit.
34. Relax . . . don't sweat the small stuff.
35. Get plenty of rest, eat healthy, exercise regularly.
36. Laugh a lot.
37. Balance your time across all aspects of your life: spiritual, family, career, social, physical, mental, financial.
38. Practice self-discipline.

39. Take time for yourself—time to dream, time to relax, time to live.

We have prepared a special poster, "Tips for Becoming a Top Time Master." This poster is based on the categories described in the Time-Management Profile you developed in Chapter Thirteen. It summarizes the key time-management concepts outlined. This is an excellent way to keep reminding yourself to develop good time-managment habits. If you'd like more information on how to get a free copy of our poster, please contact:

Dr. Merrill Douglass
Time Management Center
1401 Johnson Ferry Road, Suite 328-D6
Marietta, GA 30062
Tel: 404-973-3977

Index

Eliot, Robert, on stress management, 136
entropy, 22
essentials, 3–4
evaluation, of change, 177
Executive Soundview Book
    Summaries, 99
exercise
    procrastination and, 126, 128
    relaxation, 145–146
    stress and, 143–144, 145–146,
    149–150
    travel and, 122, 123

facsimile transmittal, 98, 108, 109
Fast Track, 99
"fight or flight" response, 138–
    139
filing, 93
    organization and, 95–96
    setting priorities in, 94–95
flexibility, in scheduling, 71–73
floor plans, of office, 110, 111
Ford, Henry, on power of
    thought, 6, 183
Franklin, Benjamin, on time, 151
Friday afternoon coordination
    meetings, 62–63
Future Shock (Toffler), 7, 140

General Electric, 58
goals, 9–20
    achievable, 156–159
    activities and, 49
    in daily plans, 63–65
    deadlines and, 13–14, 16, 17
    importance of setting, 10
    long-range, 14–16, 18–20, 54–
    55
    paperwork and, 88
    personal, 29–31, 152–153, 156–
    160
    priorities and, 11, 24–29
    professional, 29–31

in scheduling, 72
short-range, 14–16, 54–55
SMART, 16–18
value of, 11–13
in weekly plans, 58–63
worksheet for, 18–20
written, 13, 18–20

habitual behavior, 33
    changing, 171–177
    procrastination as, 126–127
    success as, 181–182
Harris, Sidney, on winners and
    losers, 9
*Helping Employees Cope with
    Change* (Truell), 148
Henry, Robert, on planning, 51
Hilton Hotels, 7
Hodgetts, Richard M., on effectiveness vs. success, 29–31
Holmes, Thomas, on stress
    measurement, 140–142
Hoover, Herbert, 73
hotels, working at, 116, 122–123

Iacocca: An Autobiography (Iacocca), 58
Iacocca, Lee, on planning, 58
ideal time, 155–156
important-urgent matrix, 26–28
indecision, procrastination and,
    132–133
interruption log, 43, 103
interruptions, 93, 102–112
    analyzing, 43, 103–104
    attitude toward, 103–107, 111–
    112
    controlling, 103, 104–105, 111–
    112
    distractions, 110–111
    effective communication and,
    107
    grouping activities for, 105–
    106